Innovation in Teaching of Research Methodology Excellence Awards 2024

An Anthology of Case Histories

Edited by Dan Remenyi

Innovation in the Teaching of Research Methodology Excellence Awards 2024: An Anthology of Case Histories

Copyright © 2024 The authors

First published July 2024

All rights reserved. Except for the quotation of short passages for the purposes of critical review, no part of this publication may be reproduced in any material form (including photocopying or storing in any medium by electronic means and whether or not transiently or incidentally to some other use of this publication) without the written permission of the copyright holder except in accordance with the provisions of the Copyright Designs and Patents Act 1988, or under the terms of a licence issued by the Copyright Licensing Agency Ltd, Saffron House, 6-10 Kirby Street, London EC1N 8TS. Applications for the copyright holder's written permission to reproduce any part of this publication should be addressed to the publishers.

Disclaimer: While every effort has been made by the editor, authors and the publishers to ensure that all the material in this book is accurate and correct at the time of going to press, any error made by readers as a result of any of the material, formulae or other information in this book is the sole responsibility of the reader. Readers should be aware that the URLs quoted in the book may change or be damaged by malware between the time of publishing and accessing by readers.

Note to readers: Some papers have been written by authors who use the American form of spelling and some use the British. These two different approaches have been left unchanged.

ISBN: 978-1-917204-03-3 (PDF)

ISBN: 978-1-917204-02-6 (Printed book)

Published by: Academic Conferences International Limited, Reading, RG4 9AY, United Kingdom, info@academic-conferences.org

Available from www.academic-bookshop.com

Table of Contents

Table of Contents	i
Acknowledgements	iii
Judging Team	iii
Introduction	v

Fears or Opportunities: Teaching Focus Group as a Qualitative Research Method

   Bingbing Ge   1

Using Action Learning and Reflective Dires for Large PG Business Research Methods Classes in Management Education.

   Ketty Grishikashvili   8

How ChatGPT became my co-lecturer

   Sophie Hieke   25

Infographics as Research Tool - to Clarify ideas, for Categorization, Iterations, Reflections and as Interaction tool

   Line Kolås, Oddlaug Marie Lindgaard and Ninni Anita Rotmo Olsen   41

Empowering Future Generations: Integrating Haptic Learning and Sustainability into University Education for Enhanced Engagement and Resilience

   Klaus Kuehnel and Manuel Au-Yong-Oliveira   59

Making Philosophy Relevant to Process and Practice: Exploring Rich Data through Assessment Journeys

   Stephen Linstead   83

A Service-learning Approach on Students Consultancy Project: Marketing Research for Breast Cancer Prevention.

Ilia Protopapa   *101*

Teaching Research Methodologies Through Participatory Performance text

Jocene Vallack   *117*

Students as Researchers: Fostering Research and Analytical Skills Through Interdisciplinary Approaches

Sandra Vasconcelos, Carla Melo, António Melo, Dália Liberato, and Maria Carlos Lopes   *129*

Acknowledgements

We would like to thank the judges, who initially read the abstracts of the case histories submitted to the competition and discussed these to select those to be submitted as full case histories. They subsequently evaluated the entries and made further selections to produce the finalists who are represented in this book.

Judging Team

Dr Martin Rich is Senior Lecturer in Information Management and Course Director for the BSc in Business Studies at Cass Business School. He has over twenty years of experience in building innovative approaches to teaching and learning into an established business school. Some of this centres around the possibilities opened by technological innovation and changes in the tools and online resources available to students to support their studies. He is also interested in how management education should evolve to meet the requirements of a changing business environment, and how students can best learn the skills and analytical techniques that will prepare them for a future that cannot be predicted. Martin's approach to learning places a strong emphasis on developing students' abilities as independent researchers, and on building ties between research methods and the abilities that business and management graduates can be expected to demonstrate during their careers. He is a regular participant in the ECRM track on teaching research methods and has published and presented around the subject.

Professor Anthony Mitchell PhD, DIC, MSc, BSc, CEng, FIET, FHEA is Professor of Operations Management at Ashridge Executive Education, Hult International Business School and a visiting fellow at Southampton University Business School. Following an early career in industry and consulting he spent 27 years at

Ashridge Business School as a senior member of faculty including MBA director and director of postgraduate projects. Anthony has held visiting roles at Monash, Otago, EIPM, RSM and Strathclyde Business school and now has an adjunct role at Ashridge. He has taught and published in the fields of operations, continuous improvement, supply chain, strategic management and eLearning. His research interests include multinational organisations, globalisation, the role of outsourcing and offshoring, and mixed methods research methodologies.

Dr José Manuel Azevedo has been a Lecturer in the Mathematics Department of ISCAP/ Polytechnic Institute of Porto (P.PORTO) since 1998. He obtained is PhD in Education (Mathematics) at the University of Beira Interior, Covilhã, Portugal. He published several articles in conferences and journals. He is a member of the program committee of some conferences in his areas of research. In addition, he also serves as a reviewer for some conferences. He supervises master students in related areas of his research interests. Researcher at CEOS.PP Research Center. His research interests are Analytics, Mathematics Education, E-Assessment, Financial Mathematics, Financial Time Series, Data Mining and E-Learning.

Introduction

The Innovation in the Teaching of Research Methods Excellence Awards is an established annual event.

We continue to be encouraged by the interest which has been shown in these Excellence Awards, as we believe that the case histories recorded here are a valuable asset to those who are trying to improve their teaching of research methodology in the social sciences.

Initially 18 submissions were received, and 9 contenders were invited to submit a full case history describing their initiative. These case histories were double-blind peer reviewed, and this publication contains the entries of the shortlisted contestants. We are once again pleased to see the global reach these Awards have with contributions this year from Australia, Germany, Norway, Portugal and the United Kingdom.

We feel that these case histories provide helpful insights into the types of issues academics are coping with when teaching research methodology today in various parts of the world.

Dan Remenyi

Editor

July 2024

dan.remenyi@academic-publishing.org

Fears or Opportunities: Teaching Focus Group as a Qualitative Research Method

Bingbing Ge
Lancaster University Management School, UK
b.ge1@lancaster.ac.uk

1. Introduction

Focus groups, as one of the unique qualitative research methods, can seem "deceptively simple' (Wilkinson, 2011:168). After all, if one can conduct a one-to-one interview, how hard could it be to do a 'group interview'1? On the contrary, it is one of the least favored qualitative research methods in my qualitative research methods for PhDs at Lancaster University Management School, UK. When teaching this method, students generally report a fear of conducting focus groups in their qualitative data collection. "Difficult to co-ordinate" and "group management" are amongst the top concerns leading to avoidance of using this method.

However, as a qualitative researcher, I recognize that properly conducted focus groups yield inherent values on phenomena like understanding group dynamics (e.g., decision-making in Top Management Teams) and empowering invisible voices (Silverman, 2020). Moreover, focus group, as a qualitative method, equips students with professional skills including communication, facilitation, and critical thinking, while enhancing their interdisciplinary understandings.

---

[1] Ryan et al., (2014) regards focus group as a "particular type of group interview where the moderator (or researcher/evaluator) asks a set of targeted questions designed to elicit views about a specific topic" (p 2).

In light of these considerations, I regard focus group as one of the important qualitative research methods for PhD students to learn about. Accordingly, over the past two years, I designed and implemented interactive role-play workshops for my PhD research methods module, allowing the students to experience the method.

2. The Lesson Plan

The interactive role-play workshop provides the students with a simulated focus group experience within a two-hour workshop, following a lecture on different qualitative research methods (including interviews, focus groups, observations, and documentation). As this lesson does not require any extra resources (e.g., software or technology), it is easily implementable across different universities. This process includes four stages: discussion of the method, warming-up and role-assigning, focus group research (role-playing), and reflections from each participant.

First stage: discussion of the method (15-20 minutes) The workshop starts with a discussion of the key issues with the focus group method, drawing together learnings through the lecture, research methodology literature, as well as students' own experiences. Students are encouraged to critically reflect on the advantages and disadvantages of the method, and on strategies for addressing potential issues/challenges. Combined with this reflective element, this teaching plan is extremely flexible and adaptive, allowing the lecturers to customize the discussions for each student cohort's specific "fears".

Next stage: warming-up and role-assigning (10 minutes) After the discussions, I have the class warm up on a particular topic, which is often a contemporary issue that is familiar and engaging for the student cohort, such as the release of a new smartphone. The students are then given the time to research and familiarize themselves with the topic individually. During their research time, I initiate the role-play. I typically have about 7-10 students in one group, running in parallel in two or three groups depending on the class sizes. The roles for each include *one researcher, participants without roles*, and *participants with roles*. The "roles" are designed to reflect typical group dynamics that students might have fears about - the enthusiastic, the shy, and the uninterested. In particular, students who are 'enthusiastic' are instructed to be disruptively enthusiastic; namely, they would try to dominate the conversation and speak off track. Students who are 'shy' are instructed to avoid eye contact and speak only short one-word answers. Students who are 'uninterested' simply act like they want to leave, and try not to engage with the topic. The roles can be flexible and reflect the outcomes from discussions at the first stage. Combined with 3-6 students who have no roles, this simulates a real-life-like focus group with interesting dynamics, also leaving room for other unprescribed dynamics.

Third stage: role play (30-45 minutes) During this phase, the students participate in their focus group simulation that mimics real-world conditions. The student, who assumes the researcher role, opens the research with typical activities using discussed 'good practices for a focus group'[2]. They are then left to run their focus group. During this stage, I walk around the class, observe the groups, and take notes for the last stage. It is worth noting that, with clear roles, all the students engage with the activity very well. I have not encountered a situation in which I needed to intervene.

Last stage: reflections (30 minutes) The workshop concludes with a reflective session, during which I would invite students to reflect on their observations. Starting from the researchers, who are invited to reflect on the group dynamics. The other students (with no roles) are then invited to provide third-party observation of the group dynamics. The role-playing participants are then invited to discuss potential strategies to deal with group dynamics, related to their roles. I conclude the session with my observations and suggestions, linking to the opening discussions in the first stage.

---

[2] In the lecture, we discuss the importance of 'setting the scene' so the participants are aware of the basic information, including self-introduction, the expectations, purpose of the research, length of the research, etc.

3. The challenges

An unexpected challenge I encountered was the requirement for acting. At times, students might fail to act in their roles due to the obligations they feel from their peers. Other times, students are not suitable for the roles. As I kept roles secretive and simply asked for volunteers, I sometimes had very enthusiastic students in the 'shy' role, or verse visa, which made the role-playing additionally difficult. To overcome this, I adapted the role assignment to be more flexible based on the characteristics of the students in the second year of teaching.

Another (potential) challenge is the relationship between the peers, as some role characteristics might irritate students in their groups. This could undermine both the purpose of the activity as well as potentially their relationship. To overcome this potential challenge, lesson planning takes this into consideration. At the warming-up (stage 2) and during the reflections (stage 4), I spent some time talking to the students, making sure that they were clear that the 'irritating' actions were designed elements that were acted out well. In so doing, I made sure that no tension was held among the groups after the activity.

4. Learner reflections

Students have generally had an idea about their preferred research methods before joining the module. Through this interactive activity, the students have reported a significant enhancement in their understanding and appreciation of focus groups as a research method, including its strength (in terms of the suitability to particular aspects of organizational life), the skillsets they need to develop to utilize it effectively, and potential challenges and strategies to handle them. While some students still have reservations about using the research methods for their research, they have a realistic understanding of the methods that they perhaps would not otherwise have.

This activity is usually done with students from a range of different cohorts and academic disciplines. I have found that students from different backgrounds articulate different gains from the activity. For example, some students from a traditional marketing research background have considered using the method before the lesson. They reflect that they are much more confident in combining this into their research planning as one of the research methods.

Other students, from an economics background, for example, have never considered using this method due to their quantitative research design. It is their first experience with a simulation of qualitative research method. This enables them to understand the qualitative research assumptions and utilizations. One student reflected that this could be useful for policy-related research, allowing better linkage with real-world impact.

A third type of student, from an entrepreneurship research background, for example, normally plans to use qualitative interviews and observation (or ethnography) in their PhD research. They reported a better appreciation of the purpose of focus groups and their potential to unpack particular dynamics in organizations.

Overall, this activity allows students with various backgrounds from diverse business management disciplines to broaden their methodological repertoire, enhance their research competence, encourage peer learning and experiential learning, and add to their personal and professional development.

5. Plans to further develop the initiative

To fully develop this activity and link it with the research module, I will carefully consider the experience in the past two years, taking into consideration the various factors, students' needs, and learning outcomes. The next step in developing the teaching is to link the topic closely with the students. I will invite the students to design the focus group in advance, as preparation for the workshop.

Additionally, I will explore successful teaching initiatives implemented by other programs in other institutions or schools for inspiration and ideas.

While different students might have different plans for their preferred research methods, I will clarify and emphasize the potential of focus groups not simply as a research method but as a professional development method. The reflection discussions will be connected more to their planned research methods and how they might work together to complement their PhD research or impact activities.

Unexpectedly, the activity works well as a team-building activity amongst the new students, allowing them to establish rapport, and creating a peer-learning environment. Therefore, it might work better at an earlier stage of the module rather than at the end.

References

Ryan, K., Gandha, T., Culbertson, M. and Carlson, C. (2014) 'Focus group evidence: implications for design and analysis', American Journal of Evaluation, 35 (3): 328-345

Silverman, D. (Ed.). (2020). Qualitative Research. London: Sage.

Wilkinson, S. (2011) 'Focus Group Research', in D. Silverman (ed.), *Qualitative Research*, third edition. London: Sage, pp. 168-184.

Author Biography

Bingbing Ge is a Lecturer at Lancaster University Management School. Her research focuses on family business management, entrepreneurship, and strategy. In particular, she looks into the role of knowledge, history, and stories in the family business entrepreneurial journey. She also contributes to knowledge exchange projects, including development and delivery of the Family Business Excellence Programme and Global Family Business Learning Symposium, and collaboration with Entrepreneurs in Residence (in Department of Entrepreneurship and Strategy).

Using Action Learning and Reflective Dires for Large PG Business Research Methods Classes in Management Education.

Dr Ketty Grishikashvili
University of Hertfordshire, Business School. Hatfield, UK
k.grishikashvili@herts.ac.uk.

1. Introduction (to the specific objectives of the initiative)

In a rapidly changing business environment, Research Methods (RM) and their application to real-world problems are becoming skills that equipped students for the rest of their lives. However, there are ongoing debates about several practical and pedagogical challenges on how to teach and assess the RM. The teaching of RM is a part of the curriculum in most of Business and Management (B&M) Postgraduate courses, as most of the master's degrees include a research project, leading to the production of a dissertation. B&M postgraduates are challenged by selecting their research topic, formulating their research aim, objectives, and potential research questions, writing the literature review, and selecting an appropriate research design for their research proposals and final projects (Wang and Li, 2008; Nielsen, 2016; Saeed et al, 2020). Saeed et al, (2020) observed that, although RM courses/modules are compulsory, many postgraduates joining masters' programmes do not have adequate experience in writing a good research proposal. Thus, majority of students joining the RM courses/modules are often found anxious, rigid to the courses and hold negative attitudes towards RM learning (Earley, 2014). These issue and challenges are becoming more an intimidating task for international postgraduates with insufficient experience in academic writing in English (Wang and Li, 2008).

One of the questions to address above mentioned challenges is how to make RM interesting to B&M students by introducing innovative and inclusive methods for learning, teaching, and assessment. Addressing this issue becomes even more debatable for the large class seatings in an increasingly internationalised context. This is not a single institution's problem in the UK, as according to the Higher Education Statistics Agency (HESA) UK, (HESA, 2023), while EU and domestic enrolment numbers saw a decrease in 2021/22, non-EU first year enrolments rose by 32% in HE. This increase was driven by a large increase in the number of first year students from non-EU countries enrolling onto postgraduate taught courses. B&M is one of the most popular degree choices among these postgraduate taught courses. Thus, specific objectives for the presented case below was:

Objective 1: To introduce an innovative and inclusive methods for learning, teaching, and assessment of Business Research Methods (BRM) Module for one of the largest B&M master's taught courses in one of the UK's higher education institutions.

The course has a very complex structure with three different (one year, sandwich/placement and advanced research) entry routes and multiple intakes (September and January) with approximately 2000 new students for per academic year.

In this B&M masters course students are required to join several compulsory modules, one of which is the BRM. The BRM module is a 15-credit module designed to empower students develop postgraduate level skills of independent research. In particular, aim of the module is to enable students to: (1) identify a contemporary business and/or management issue to formulate research topic, (2) identify relevant literature, providing critical analysis of the theories, (3) understand relevant methodological concepts and challenges associated with business research, (4) formulate an appropriate ethical research strategy to plan the gathering and analysis of appropriate data (5) formulate a research proposal on a particular topic of students' interest. The BRM module is crucial on this course, as it is not only equipping students with the essential research related skills but also it forms a solid foundation for the final masters' research project.

Majority of students on the course are international students with diverse educational and cultural background. Diversity management in classrooms requires a range of instructions to be set and followed, as a lack of competencies in managing diverse classroom environments can increase behavioural issues and it also affect students' academic performance (Milner et al, 2014). Thus, creating an inclusive and positive learning environment, monitoring attendance and engagement same time as making BRM module interesting for international students in large class settings was another challenge on this course/module. Therefore, second objective of this case was:

Objective 2: To make BRM module interesting for international students in large class settings, by creating inclusive environment, increasing engagement, and improving attendance.

Research (Earley, 2014, Ellis and Goodyear 2016, Rich et al., 2019, Saeed et al., 2020) and evidence from practice suggest, that incorporating active and action learning strategies for those involved in teaching large classes might be a solution to overcome above mention challenges. It has been recommended, that teaching, learning and assessment, which puts students in charge of their own learning through participation in activities (active learning) coupled with encouraging students to work with their peers as a 'set' (action learning) increase their participation and engagement. Using this strategy believed to be beneficial especially for those groups where there is a diversity, for example, in terms of prior knowledge and/or cultural and learning experiences.

Active learning refers to student-centred approach that emphasises learners' engagement in active and meaningful construction of their learning (Yao and Collins 2018). The key idea behind active learning and student engagement is reflecting on the experience of learning by doing (Chickering and Gamson 1987; Gibbs 1998; Healey, et. al.,2010). Active engagement in learning may take different forms: flipped classrooms, internship, group discussions collaborative assignments and project, problem solving approach, case study, business simulations, subject-based research, and inquiry etc.

With a small difference form active learning, action learning could be defined as a process that involves a small group working on real problems, taking action, and learning as individuals, as a team, and as an organisation. Action learning necessarily occurs in a closed group or 'set' and, while individuals in the set may each have their own unique problem to work on, learning occurs via the interaction between members of the 'set' (Revans, 2011).

2. The infrastructure, (i. e. people, systems, exercises, or perhaps hardware, software if any)

The innovative methods employed in this module were to address the above-mentioned objectives, making BRM more interesting for B&M students by creating inclusive environment, increasing engagement, and improving attendance. While managing large courses and modules, it emerged from the module leaders' practice who is the author of this case and discussed introduced methods, that engagement is driven through interaction and participation. Best way to remain students engaged, especially in an internationalised setting is to keep session interactive. This was achieved by incorporating active and action learning strategies in flipped classroom settings. Flipped classroom settings consistent with research-informed/led practice were deployed and flanked by a Learning Set Conversation (LSC) and Reflection to ensure that different students' learning needs and preferences were met, regardless of their learning styles, abilities, and backgrounds. For the visual image please see the appendix 1.

The idea was to create an inclusive and interactive environment where students could master technical and theoretical information through LSC, reflection, and critical analysis. The module was taught by the module leader and tutors (between seven to twelve depending on intake) in approximately fifteen separate groups (depending on intake) during the first semester for each intake between 2021-2022 and 2022-2023 years. All tutors on the module were experience staff and had different competencies and expertise in BRM.

Approximate number of students for each group was between 50-60. As part of the assessment during the first four weeks' tutorial sessions students were asked to prepare for and participate in a LSC (an approximately 30 minutes) which was facilitated by tutor. In every tutorial, tutors were forming a Learning Set within their tutorial groups, with a minimum of four and maximum of five members. As a Learning Set, seated in a circular arrangement student were exploring case studies and key issues associated with the contemporary B&M research practices with their peers. Facing each other, making eye contact, and engaging in a meaningful discussion, breaks down barriers and promotes active participation, as every student has an equal opportunity to contribute and be heard. After each LSC, each member of Learning Set was asked to reflect on their LSC and produce a Reflective Piece of Work Reflective Diaries (RD) no more than 250 words and no less than 150, which was assessed as part of the module assessments.

The syllabus, (which typically included: Research topic, aim and objectives; Literature review; Research design; Research and ethics; Data collection methods; Data analysis methods) course materials and tasks for assessment was same to all groups. All module related materials (PowerPoint slides, books, book chapters, case study, short videos, journal articles and assignment briefs) were uploaded and posted on the module's Canvas site.

The module delivery structure included: (1) Preparation stage: Pre-class self-study, (2) 1 hour face to face Lecture (delivered by the module leader), (3) 1 hour face to face tutorial (delivered by tutor) and (4) Strech/Post-class self-study. A new innovative assessment, the Weekly Reflective Work/ RD submission, which was based on the LSC discussion, during the tutorials, was introduced on the module since the module leader took the module leadership from previous module leaders. Using the LSC during the tutorials and Reflective Diaries (RD) for the weekly submissions, encouraged students to share their experiences - good and bad - and reflect together to draw out the learning. The learning came not only from lecturer/tutors bringing new information or insight (which normally is done during the lecture), but from the members of the LSC sharing their experiences and reflecting on it. Having, LSC about the case study, which was linked to the week's topic, helped students to adopt multicultural environment and have a great experience as an international student. In addition, introducing the Weekly Reflective Work/RD submission as a form of assessment, helped students to keep RD, which allowed them to observe their own research practice and the lessons they have learnt.

3. The challenges (how and when they were encountered, how they were overcome)

It has been argued (Earley, 2014, Lewthwaite and Nind, 2016) that research methods courses (modules) are the most intellectually demanding than subject matter courses because they require students to seize a complex abstract principles and processes. The capacity to undertake and engage with research requires a combination of theoretical understanding, procedural knowledge and mastery of a range of practical skills' (Kilburn et al., 2014, p. 191). Thus, very often students on these courses are concerned about their inability to understand difficult and abstract concepts related to RM (Howard and Brady, 2015). On the other hand, teaching BRM is complicated because students often come from a wide range of disciplines, with different prior knowledge, diverse interests, and expectations, as such, employing a pedagogical approach that appeals to all students is difficult to achieve (Daniel, 2017). In addition, students' engagement always been a problem for us during the pandemic online settings or now in face-to-face environment. Bringing students back to campus, monitoring attendance and engagement while adopting a post pandemic became an increasingly challenging in the education system. Using the LSC during the tutorials and Reflective Diaries (RD) for the weekly submissions helped to overcome above mention challenges. Having LSC during the tutorials as part of weekly assessment helped to improve an engagement, attendance, and an interaction on the module. Please see below for further details.

4. How the initiative was received by the users or participants

Majority of students reported that the BRM module had effective structure. Having flipped class settings helped students to access the module content including recorded lectures outside of face-to-face class time (during "*Preparation*" stage pre-class self-study and "*Strech*" post-class self-study). As a result, students could review case studies and other course materials in advance to tutorial then have class sessions for working together on the assignments.

The LSC during the tutorials also was acknowledged to be effective way of delivering the BRM module. Having LSC during the tutorials as part of weekly assessment helped to improve an engagement and an interaction on the module. In addition, as some of the students indicated it helped them to bullied interest in RM.

> *S1[2021 Sem A intake]: Having LSC in class and being more interactive has helped me build interest in BRM. This is the first time I have taken this course. So, I don't know how to do research and I was very sceptical about it.*

> *S2[2021 Sem A intake]: The lectures and tutorial has been very insightful and impactful. The Canvas App made the learning experience quite easy and seamless.. Access to reading materials and textbook online was very helpful. Lecturer and Tutors are excellent!*

> *S3[2022 Sem B Intake]: The tutorial sessions, LSC, have been very great it is helped me understand BRM to a very large extent, weekly reflection has helped me to develop ability of critical thinking about the case study have discussed and studied.*

> *S4[2022 Sem A Intake]: Having this type of BRM lesson makes me very happy. It provided me with many answers to my problems, greatly aided in the advancement of my profession, and increased my understanding and comprehension of business research.*

S5[2023 Sem B intake]: It is very interesting to have LSC about the case studies in tutorials. It helps to gain knowledge regarding the final project and assignments. The case studies discussions with other classmates helps to gain a lot of knowledge. Enjoying the module.

S6[2023 Sem A intake]: I was pretty scared in the first few weeks on how I can work on my research proposal. But as each week progressed, the lectures and tutorials made me feel confident that I can submit a good proposal. I like how the BRM module is designed to help the student understand research methods in a step by step manner.

S7[2023 Sem B intake: I loved this method of teaching. During tutorials I am able to apply many of the things taught. The lectures are also good. There is a lot of information shared from experts. I'm still getting used to this system as in my home country there's a lot of learning happening inside the class n less personal work. When it comes to BRM I am happy because I thought it wouldn't be a great journey with this module, but it is

Positive feedback was also about the Reflective Work/Reflective Diaries submission from all cohorts. The research process is usually presented as a sequence of between seven and ten distinct stages all of which must be completed for any piece of research to be credible (Saunders et al, 2019). It is easy to get lost in necessary details, required to successfully carry out the individual steps. By taking each step separately, and design weekly units/topics based on Business Research Methods textbook (Saunders et al, 2019) lectures, weekly LSC and Reflective Work/ Reflective Diaries submission tend to support this outcome. Having Reflective Diaries helped students to iterate between these steps, perhaps revisiting various stages many times, as their understanding of the research problem develops and changes as a result of the findings from other steps such as literature review or research design.

S8[2021 Sem A intake]: BRM Tutorial was very interesting and weekly reflection report helped to think critically and how apply theory to research.

S9[2022 Sem B Intake]: weekly reflection in the module was a great idea as it helps to remember what we learnt in the lecture and tutorial.

S10[2022 Sem A Intake]: Sessions are really good and I am able to catch what tutors are teaching in class. By the weekly reflection assignments we could learn more deeply about the subject and it helps me to prepare a basement for my final research.

S11[2023 Sem B intake]: This module has been helpful in many ways as a post graduate student. It helped to get back to studies as many of us where joining after a break from studies. The weekly reflection helped to get back to writing to and develop research proposal.

S12[2023 Sem A intake]: Excellent. The Module has been helpful in giving us a clear understanding about research methods and all the processes involved in conducting a research. Weekly submissions helped us to develop our research proposal step by step.

S13[2023 Sem B intake]: I am quite happy with the module and the teaching methodology, I am able to understand everything, and my perception about the module has changed as I felt I won't be able to do well in this module, but because of my tutor ……and ….., I feel more confident and feel incredible that I am able to study this module very well..

It wasn't surprising to discover how much influence the teaching staff had on making these new methods work in practice. The module team's effort, skills, experience, and expertise were acknowledged and appreciated by students:

S14[2021 Sem A intake]: The teaching staff consistently make the subject engaging by incorporating interactive discussions, real-world examples, and multimedia resources, fostering active participation and deeper understanding among students throughout the module.

S15[2022 Sem B Intake]: The module staff frequently stimulate intellectual curiosity, inspiring further study through thought-provoking discussions, challenging assignments, and insightful content, motivating students to delve deeper into the subject matter.

S16[2022 Sem A Intake]: The module leader and tutors maintain a balanced approach, providing clear guidance for directed study while encouraging independent exploration and critical thinking, ensuring students develop both skills effectively.

S17[2023 Sem B intake]: Feedback from staff consistently aids improvement by providing actionable insights and constructive suggestions during teaching sessions, and assessments, enhancing understanding and refining skills for continuous academic development.

S18[2023 Sem A intake]: The module teaching staff have been extremely supportive, promptly addressing inquiries, offering assistance when needed, and guiding towards additional support resources, greatly enhancing my learning experience.

S19[2023 Sem A intake]: Students' opinions are highly valued by staff, demonstrated through active solicitation of feedback, attentiveness to concerns, and willingness to incorporate suggestions, fostering a collaborative and supportive learning environment.

S20[2023 Sem B intake]: The module effectively prepared me for assessments by providing comprehensive content, practical guidance, and valuable feedback, equipping me with the necessary knowledge and skills to succeed in evaluations.

4.1 Data collection & Ethical Consideration

Please note that effectiveness of the introduced methods and recommendations are based on Mid-module feedback which was taken from 3 different intakes between 2021-2023. As this study was taken purely for the pedagogical reasons and is not conceived as pure research at this stage study didn't go through the ethical approval.

> *According to Universities policy "Protocol for Reflective Practitioner Work by Academic Staff" - The intention of a tutor who reflects on the curriculum, how it operates, how it matches the students' needs and expectations and the requirements of external bodies and so on, is simply to update and/or improve the curriculum in the interests of doing what the University is charged to do: providing a curriculum that is current and comparable to that offered at other institutions. This is normal professional practice and is undertaken with purely pedagogical concerns in mind. The tutor has no research agenda in mind at the time and it is important that this professional updating should proceed without any tutor thinking that it should be inhibited by ethical considerations. Assuming that what happens to the students as a result of the changes continues to be ethical in a broad sense, there is no need to apply for ethical approval for them. The distinction to be made is that that the changes were made by the tutor in the interest of improving the module and the student experience and not in the interest of carrying out a piece of research. (UPR RE01, 2021).*

In addition, Mid -module feedback on the module was collected anonymously online settings (via Padlet) without confirming any personal data. Questions, or any other aspect of the procedure, didn't intrude on the student's privacy, or risk upsetting or disturbing the students in any way. Innovative approach discussed above is reported at both informal and formal discussions and conferences both within and outside the university *(UPR RE01, 2021)*.

5. The learning outcomes (What was achieved and how the outcomes were measured/evaluated)

On top of the benefits discussed above it must be acknowledged that, after implementing new innovative teaching learning and assessment methods for the BRM module, according to the Module Evaluation Form (MEF)s, overall failure rate on the module dropped nearly 70% and attendance and engagement improved dramatically. According to tutors working on the module, introduced new method for teaching, learning and assessment helped them to build a good relationship with students, which on the other hand helped to improve interest in RM and improve attendance and engagement. The module team noted that quality of the final proposals improved, and rate of plagiarism cases decreased. The BRM module's learning outcomes as listed below were achieved. Students were prepared better for the final MSc projects as they were able to:

- Understand relevant methodological concepts and challenges associated with business research,
- Critically examine the range of research methods and justify their potential relevance to a chosen research topic,
- Analyse ethical aspects of research design and propose responsible research.

In addition, introduced innovative teaching learning and assessment methods helped students to develop, intellectual, practical and transferable skills such as:

- Identify relevant literature, providing critical analysis of the theories, concepts, paradigms, and views,
- Formulate an appropriate ethical research strategy to plan the gathering and analysis of appropriate data,
- Propose a complex research activity in a systematic and creative manner.

6. Plans to further develop the initiative.

Evidence presented in this case, which is only very small part of data large data, indicates that integrating action and active learning strategies in BRM module was effective strategy which improved overall modules performance and students' perception about the BRM. It is an intention of the author to introduce the same methods for the dissertation module, as it could be assumed that having Learning Set Conversations and Reflective Diaries can be a great tool to evaluate a teaching and learning on the research related modules. This is an effective way to reflect on the research process e.g. noting whether the research methods are appropriate and useful, whether identified literature is sufficient or any bias during the data collection. In addition, using same methods for the dissertation module will allow B&M students to observe their own research practice and the lessons they have learnt.

References

Chickering, A. W. and Gamson, Z. F. (1987). Seven principles for good practice in undergraduate education. American Association for Higher Education Bulletin.

Daniel, B. K. (2019). Improving the Pedagogy of Research Methodology through Learning Analytics. The Electronic Journal of Business Research Methods. Vol. 17 (1).

Earley, M. (2014). A synthesis of the literature on research methods education, Teaching in Higher Education. Vol. 19 (3), pp. 242-253.

Ellis, R. A., and P. Goodyear. (2016). Models of Learning Space: Integrating Research on Space, Place and Learning in Higher Education. Review of Education 4 (2), pp. 49- 191.

Gibbs, G. (1998). Control and independence. in Gibbs, G. and Jenkins, A. (eds.) Teaching large classes in higher education: How to maintain quality with reduced resources. London: Kogan, pp. 37-59.

Gibbs, A., and Jenkins, G. (1992). Teaching Large Classes in Higher Education: Kogan Page Limited.

Healey, M. and Jenkins, A. (2009). Developing undergraduate research and inquiry. York: Higher Education.

Healey, M., Bovill, C. and Jenkins, A. (2010). Students as partners in learning, in Lea, J. (Ed.) Enhancing learning and teaching in higher education: Engaging with the dimensions of practice. Maidenhead: Open University Press.

Kilburn, D., Nind, M. and Wiles, R. (2014). Learning as researchers and teachers: the development of a pedagogical culture for social science research methods? British Journal of Educational Studies. Vol. 62 (2), pp. 191-207.

Lewthwaite, S., and Nind, M. (2016). Teaching research methods in the social sciences: experts' perspectives on pedagogy and practice', British Journal of Educational Studies. Vol. 64 (4), pp. 413-430.

Milner, H, R, and Blake F, T. (2014). Classroom Management in Diverse Classrooms. Urban Education. Vol. 45, (5). Available at: https://doi.org/10.1177/0042085910377290.

Nielsen, B. B, Eden, L and Verbeke, A. (2016). Research Methods in International Business: Challenges and Advances. Research Methods in International Business.

Rich, M.G. (2014). Learning Research Methods: How Personalised Should we be? Electronic Journal of Business Research Methods, 12 (2), pp. 131-138.

Revans, R.W. (2011). Action Learning London: Chartwell Bratt.

Saeed. M. A, Ahdal, M.H and Al Qunayeer, H. (2020). Integrating research proposal writing into a postgraduate research method course: what does it tell us? International Journal of Research & Method in Education. Vol. 44 (3), pp. 303-318.

Saeed. M. A, and Al Qunayeer, H. (2020). Can we engage postgraduates in active research methodology learning? Challenges, strategies and evaluation of learning. International Journal of Research & Method in Education. Vol. 44 (1), pp. 1-19.

Sunders, M, Lewis, P and Thornhil, A. (2019). Research Methods for Business Students. Pearson Education Limited.

The Higher Education Statistics Agency (HESA) UK. (2023) Available at: https://www.hesa.ac.uk/data-and-analysis/students/what-study.

University of Hertfordshire (2021) Protocol for Reflective Practitioner Work by Academic Staff. Available at: https://www.herts.ac.uk/__data/assets/pdf_file/0003/233643/RE01-Apx1-Protocol-Reflective-Practitioner-work-by-Academic-Staff-v12.0.pdf

Wang, T and Li, Y.L. (2014). Understanding International Postgraduate Research Students' Challenges and Pedagogical Needs in Thesis Writing. International Journal of Pedagogies and Learning Vol. 4 (3).

Yao, C. W., and C. Collins. 2018. "Perspectives From Graduate Students on Effective Teaching Methods: a Case Study From a Vietnamese Transnational University." Journal of Further and Higher Education 43 (7), pp. 1-16.

Appendix 1. Visual image of discussed case.

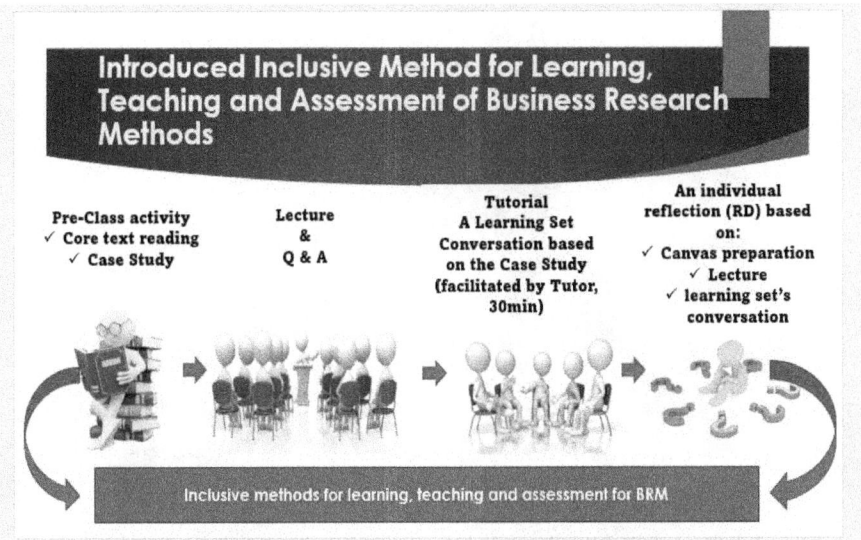

Author Biography

Ketty Grishikashvili is currently a Principal lecturer in Strategic Management at the University of Hertfordshire Business School where I am also the Associate Head (scholarship) of Strategic Management Department. Beside other scholarly activities I am leading the Business Research Methods (with 900+ students for each semester) (level 7) module. My research interest and expertise are in the broad area of Strategic Management with a particular interest in Big Data and required Resources and Capabilities/ Dynamic Capabilities as well as Research Methods/ Business Research Method and Action learning: managing large PG classes.

Ketty Grishikashvili

Current The BRM Module Team

How ChatGPT became my co-lecturer

Sophie Hieke
Munich Business School, Elsenheimerstrasse, Munich, Germany
sophie.hieke@munich-business-school.de

1. Introduction

1.1   Why Teach Critical Thinking?

Critical thinking is considered one of the key skills needed in contemporary societies, with the UN and UNESCO having gone as far as identifying it as a requirement for achieving the Sustainable Development Goals (SDG) (Andreucci-Annunziata et al., 2023). Developing such thinking skills has therefore become a priority for educational institutions, particularly higher education, not least because of their goal to develop responsible citizens (Behar-Horenstein & Niu, 2011) and answer to their calling as change agents who prepare leaders of the future to effect such SDG change (Deo et al., 2023; Spanjol et al., 2023).

How to effectively teach critical thinking, however, is a more complicated matter and criticism has centered around the notion that educational efforts are often more concentrated on "what to think rather than how to think" (Daud & Husin, 2004, p. 478).

Typically, critical thinking can be taught directly (the general approach) or indirectly, by integrating it in the subject matter (infusion approach) or resulting from students engaging in the subject matter (immersion approach) (Ennis, 1989). The indirect approach distinguishes between explicit (students know that critical thinking skills are being taught) and implicit (they are not aware of it) methods and studies have shown that infusion teaching (explicit) yields better results than immersion (implicit) (Behar-Horenstein & Niu, 2011).

Research has also looked into the right exercises for teaching critical thinking skills (Alsaleh, 2020), finding that, for example, critiquing journal articles, engaging in debates, writing research papers, evaluating case studies, and discussing questions helps to successfully develop and practice these skills (Lawrence et al., 2008). Learning objectives hence include that students can define and clarify information, ask appropriate questions, clarify or challenge statements or beliefs, judge the credibility of sources, and solve problems by predicting probable outcomes logically or through deduction (Lipman, 1988).

And so I have long designed my "Critical Thinking" course as part of our undergraduate program "International Business" according to these evidence-based recommendations. I used a combination of the general and the infusion approach, introducing students to frameworks and taxonomies around critical thinking, discussing why this skill set is important in today's times and providing them with articles they were to critically assess in class, checking sources and challenging statements and beliefs.

1.2   And Then There Was ChatGPT

When ChatGPT was released in the fall of 2022, it was clear to me that the world as we know it has changed and that this must be reflected in higher education: what we teach and particularly how we teach it. Generative AI is completely disrupting life in general, but particularly work, and if we want to prepare our students for their future and equip them with the skills they need to succeed, we must embrace this new reality rather than shut the technology out of the classroom. It may not be AI that takes away your job but it certainly will be the people who can (more) effectively use it.

While the integration of technology with critical thinking skills in higher education settings has long been called for (Calma & Davies, 2020), integration of AI in teaching methods can certainly be seen as a major shift in educational approaches (Essien et al., 2024). As of now, the education sector is considered to be lagging behind in terms of AI technology adoption, despite its potential to enhance learning and teaching (O'Dea & O'Dea, 2023). Empirical evidence on how the use of AI tools such as ChatGPT could help enhance cognitive skills is scarce but first studies are promising (Essien et al., 2024).

Five key skills have been identified as pivotal in preparing students for an AI-infused world: (1) problem formulation (identifying, analyzing and defining problems and translating these needs into a problem that generative AI tools can understand and help solve), (2) exploration (knowing which tools exist and what they can do), (3) experimentation (learning through interaction with different AI tools via trial and error), (4) evaluation (understanding the limitations of different tools and the technology overall by being able to critically assess the outcomes) and (5) reflection (openness to understand one's own emotional reactions to AI tools producing outcomes previously considered human-specific) (Acar, 2023).

As a consequence, I have taken 8 months and spent many hours in conversation with colleagues as well as external AI experts to completely redesign my approach to teaching critical thinking. I have rebuilt my course using the PAIR framework (problem formulation, AI tool selection, interaction and reflection) (Acar, 2023) and developing exercises that apply generative AI in different capacities (Mollick & Mollick, 2023), as shown in Figure 1 below.

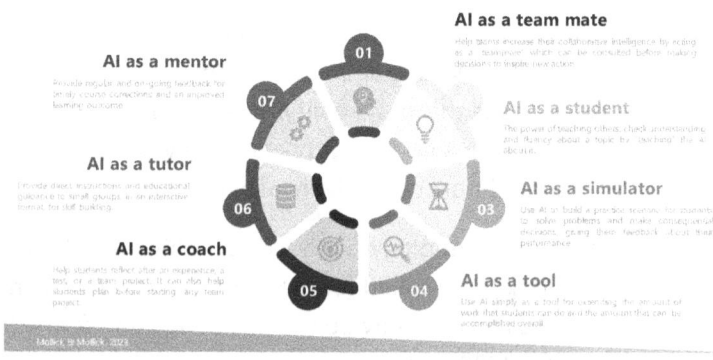

Figure 1: 7 Ways of Using AI in the classroom (Mollick & Mollick, 2023)

1.1 Meet My New Co-Lecturer

The concept of this course is to learn about different ways that generative AI can be used during studies but also beyond. The real twist, however, is that we want to help students develop their critical thinking skills when applying AI without teaching them directly, i.e., telling them what critical thinking skills are and how they must be used. Rather, students are meant to hone these skills by doing, by applying and by talking about their experiences in each class. As such, there is no typical content that is covered in this course but rather, students work on assignments using different generative AI tools and then share their experiences through class discussions. I am no longer an instructor of content but rather function as a discussion partner who asks questions but gives few answers – because often there are none as the AI world is still developing or simply because people need to form their own opinions on many topics. This is precisely the setting in which we hope that critical thinking skills are developed because students need to think for themselves and form their own viewpoints.

This course takes place in the first semester of our program and we see it as a way to ease students into their overall learning journey, followed by additional critical thinking courses in subsequent semesters, each covering other aspects and continuously building their critical thinking skills over time. Whilst we have always put a clear focus on teaching soft skills in our undergraduate program, the advent of publicly accessible generative AI tools such as ChatGPT has made this need even more urgent and it has also created new challenges that students need to deal with, from detecting fake information to creating new or fake information themselves.

2. Infrastructure

The course is split into five sessions, each dedicated to working with generative AI tools on different tasks and followed by an open discussion at the end (Figure 2). Of the 90 minutes that each class lasts, 1/3 is dedicated to this discussion, to ensure enough room for thoughts and different viewpoints.

Sophie Hieke

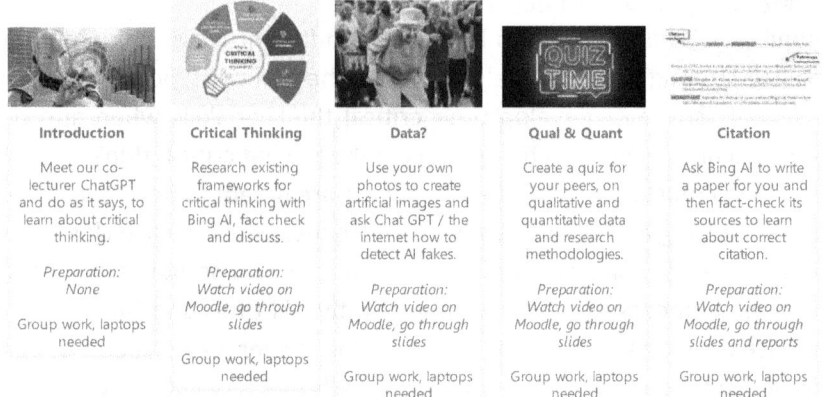

Figure 2: Overview of course/sessions

The first session starts with a deep fake video of me, telling students that they will be "taught by the AI", followed by a live session with ChatGPT in class, where we put together our first prompt on the screen, asking for case studies that students can work on in groups, to discuss the role of critical thinking in business. Students then pick one of the cases proposed by the AI and work on it, with me functioning mainly as an advisor, a sparring partner and possibly a prompt engineer. The session is closed by a discussion of their experiences, what they think about AI as a use case for building up critical thinking skills and their expectations for this class. So far, lack of knowledge as well as misconceptions on how generative AI works has been apparent in these discussions but we expect this to change slowly, over time, with students having been more exposed to these tools in the coming years.

The second session is dedicated to widening students' experiences with other generative AI tools such as Bing AI/Copilot, Gemini or Perplexity, tasking them with selecting a suitable framework on critical thinking and preparing a poster presentation on this. Again, students work in groups, with me functioning as an advisor, a sparring partner and, when necessary, as a prompt engineer. Students then present their posters and we discuss their experiences working with the AI, differences they noticed among the different AI tools and how they might be using them in their further studies when having to learn about new topics, theories or frameworks. One realization is often that students report needing to verify the information from the AI through other means such as regular web-based research, to ensure the detection of hallucations by the AI but also to read up on literature around the topic.

The third session focuses on image generation and students are asked to look up and use different tools for either generating new images or extending existing photos. They are encouraged to be creative, use different prompts such as "create this image in the style of Picasso or Banksy" but also to try and achieve realistic visuals that cannot be differentiated from "real photos" anymore. In the future, this will expand to video creation, when these tools become more widely available. The best images are then selected and showcased in class (see Figure 3 for examples), followed by a discussion on what this means for consuming visuals on the internet, e.g., on social media. Topics covered include trustworthiness of images, how to deal with fake news and what if any students can do to verify sources in their daily (and constant) consumption of media. The discussion in this session often leads to darker topics as well, including bullying and sexual harassment by creating fake porn or even child pornography. Questions around image verification and legal prosecution also come up. This session tends to be the most intense and emotionally charged one.

Figure 3: sample images created by students (artificial extension of existing photos, realistic photography, fake news)

Sophie Hieke

The fourth session opens up a new application of generative AI: helping students study for their exams. They are tasked with creating quizzes on a specific topic and these quizzes are then distributed in class, for others to take and provide feedback on. The tone of this session is more upbeat than the previous one and students are encouraged to look up fun game tools such as Kahoot in order to make this an entertaining experience. The discussion revolves around asking how they can use AI tools to help them prepare for exams, using generative AI as a study buddy. A second line of thinking is encouraged when I ask them whether they feel they learned something about their topic whilst putting together the quiz. More often than not, they start realizing that the time it took them to research the topic, select the right questions and check correct answers was actually time spent studying the topic and may be the true reason that this application of generative AI can be helpful in learning.

The last session is designed as an individual rather than a group exercise, with students being tasked to write a short seminar paper on a topic, using various generative AI tools from text generation to spell checking, and then have it graded by another student in class, also using AI. Students are then asked to share their experiences in both writing the essay and grading it, how they used AI and which of the two tasks took more time. Not surprisingly, they report that the grading was more time-intense as they had to research the topic and be context-specific in asking AI to provide feedback on the paper. They are also asked what is needed in a good prompt to receive valuable feedback from the AI and how they can use this in future assignments during their studies, to improve their output. The discussion then revolves around asking them whether they think a business school should allow students to use AI in writing, what such an AI policy should look like and what they think of the policy we have in place. I usually end this discussion with showing them my own AI policy (Figure 4) before I share their graded assignment for this course with them: a 2-page essay on how this course has shaped their view on generative AI, with an additional ½ page asking them to detail how they used AI in putting this essay together.

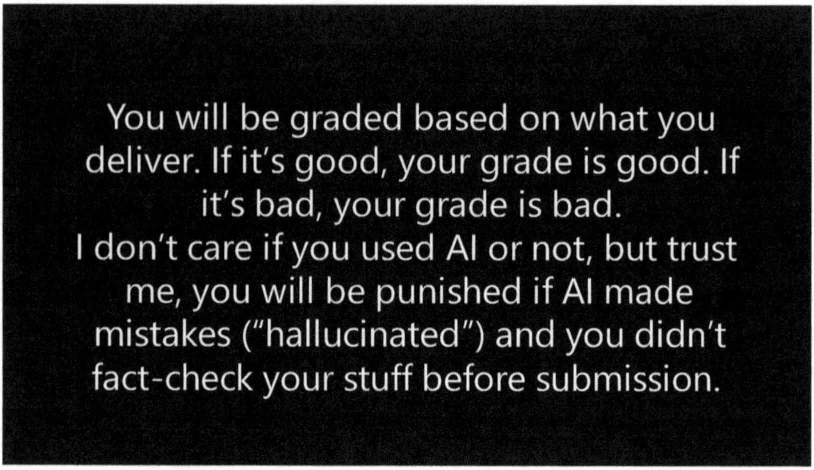

Sophie Hieke

> You will be graded based on what you deliver. If it's good, your grade is good. If it's bad, your grade is bad.
> I don't care if you used AI or not, but trust me, you will be punished if AI made mistakes ("hallucinated") and you didn't fact-check your stuff before submission.

Figure 4: AI policy for this course

The course ends with an open feedback round on what they think about this course, whether they would change anything in future courses and what they feel they have taken away from this experience.

3. Challenges

Initially, one challenge became evident when students were told at the beginning of the course that participation was not mandatory but rather at their own choice. The aim was to offer a course interesting and inspiring enough to get voluntary student participation and engagement. However, in the first semester that this course was taught (fall term 2023), the majority of students decided to not attend after the first session. This was likely instigated by one student walking out of class during the introduction. In the open feedback session at the end of the last class, students were asked what they would keep and what they would change about the course structure and the response was to make attendance mandatory as they wanted to be told what to do. When asked whether they wanted to be treated as adults or as school children, they preferred the latter, having just come out of the school system. This came as a surprise to us but when we repeated the same procedure the following semester (spring term 2024), attendance was almost at 100% for all classes. Students were again asked if they would change anything about this course and this time around, comments referring to the voluntary attendance were positive. Students appreciated having been given the choice and rather coming back because they wanted to and not because they had to. The plan is to continue this voluntary participation for a few semesters and keep track of differences across cohorts.

Another challenge lies in the fact that contrary to expectations, not all students fully understand the idea behind this course by the end of the five sessions and some complain that they don't feel they have learned anything other than how to use different generative AI tools. The working hypothesis at this point is that this learning journey likely takes longer than anticipated and its full effects won't be apparent until later in their studies, when they have more teaching formats to compare this one to and will have been able to bear the fruits of their labor by having used these new AI skills in other classes and for other assignments.

Lastly, though not a challenge that holds room for in-class learning, IT issues can make classes difficult when the internet is not working properly and hot spots on students' mobile phones don't work due to the set-up of the building where reception is often poor. A good IT infrastructure is therefore absolutely paramount for such a course.

3.1   How the initiative was received by the users or participants

Course evaluation so far has been mainly positive and some comments are provided below:

- I thought this course was very interesting. In my view, it is important to cover this topic, especially because many are not very knowledgeable on it.
- I liked how she encouraged all of us to broaden our horizon with open AI and allowed us to do a lot of things by ourselves. It was a very relaxing course as it wasn't filled with theory but rather with a lot of practice.

- Overall, the structure of the class was easy to follow. We went over the different types of AI that can be used in an academic context, applying and adapting to the innovation of AI. I have increased my knowledge in the world of AI, learning how to check the sources, verifying the research, and generating an overall better essay.
- This subject should be a very important part of our lives and this course has really given me a completely different perspective on AI etc. Thank you so much for being so passionate about it and teaching us!
- I really enjoyed attending your course and found it exciting to get a little insight into a world that is very distant to me personally. I hardly use any AI tools myself, I'm probably more of the old-school fraction that finds it creepy rather than helpful. But perhaps that's precisely the reason why I should get more involved with it instead of burying my head in the sand out of fear. To inform myself in order to overcome the uncertainty. Thanks for the insights!

In the fall term 2023 where this course took place for the first time, the overall grades using the German school grade system (where 1= very good and 5=insufficient) were 1.91 and 1.5 respectively. Two cohorts evaluated the course, one in our bilingual track (taught mainly in German) and one in the English track. In the spring term 2024, course evaluations were 2.13 and 1.6 respectively, for the English track and the bilingual track. In summary, students rate this course somewhere between very good and good.

4. Learning outcomes

We have been measuring the learning outcomes of this course via the course assignment (essay), the course evaluation (see above) and through a research project specifically created for this course.

Even with just two rounds of this course having taken place, results from the assignment already show one clear outcome: those students whose ½ page on how they used AI in writing their essay was thought through, detailed and offered new insights generally also delivered a better overall essay (2 pages on how this course helped shape their view on generative AI). This result is in line with the experience I have made in other courses I teach where I also gave students the opportunity to detail how they used AI in writing their essay. Interestingly, these courses are part of our masters' program where students are more advanced and generally more experienced both in writing and in using AI tools. It appears that this result holds true independent of the program level. These findings are very much aligned with what we already see happening in the work place where generative AI tools are used for a variety of tasks: it won't be the AI that takes away jobs but it will be people who know how to work with AI that will. And if we want to prepare our students as best possible for their later career path, we must help them learn how to use AI for their own purposes. This includes understanding what the different tools can and can't do. Additionally, when comparing results from fall 2023 to spring 2024, it has become clear that students are getting better at reflecting about the role and relevance of critical thinking in this new AI-infused world. In-class discussions already showed a steep learning curve as the new cohort has had more time to experience generative AI in their lives. Overall, results of the assignments improved in terms of quality of the essay, use of AI tools in generating the essay and reflecting on how this course has shaped their (world) view. Notably, more students explicitly chose to write the essay on their own as they wanted to express their thoughts and feelings without technology telling them what to say. Such changes across the cohorts are expected to continue over time as the development of generative AI will continue in ways we are not yet able to foresee.

In our aim to develop effective learnings strategies around soft skills such as critical thinking, we have set up a research project that accompanies this course. The main goal is to evaluate the effectiveness of this new form of teaching by using the 4 levels of training evaluation model (Kirkpatrick & Kirkpatrick 2006) and whether this leads to changes in self-reported critical thinking skills (dependent variable). Additionally, we are interested to see whether General Self-Efficacy in students moderates these effects. The measurements take place at three intervals, one right before the course, one right after it finishes and one 3-4 months later, for mid- to long-term effects.

Results are still outstanding as this project is designed as a time-series study but first insights show that the effects of this course on developing critical thinking skills need time and are not immediate. This is in line with the scholarly discussion around whether critical thinking can be taught (Calma & Davies, 2020, Behar-Horenstein & Niu, 2011), arguing that developing such skills is hard, takes practice and requires transfer across different disciplines for its mastery (van Gelder, 2005).

5. Next steps

Continuous feedback from students via the course evaluation as well as the open feedback round at the end of the last session will be used to adjust this course and its approach. It is also expected that with the advent of new generative AI tools, new assignments such as video creation or the use of GPTs, e.g., for coding, will be developed.

Additionally, a rising number of invitations to present this course and our learnings at conferences, events and particularly at other higher education institutions offers the possibility of gathering outside feedback from other lecturers, experts in the field of generative AI and audiences unrelated to teaching but for whom such a course is still relevant and interesting. Such feedback is also incorporated into the continuous adjustment of the course.

We plan on extending this course to other program levels such as graduate and post-graduate, given that the impact of generative AI on this world is relevant for all of our students. One idea currently entertained is to put together a course in the form of an online program that all students can participate in, with similar exercises and a moderated discussion forum where they can share their learnings and experiences with others. This can eventually lead to a larger, more externally available course on platforms such as Coursera.

Inspired by feedback from external speaking events, we are also considering setting up workshop formats with staff and faculty designed to foster critical thinking no matter the stage of your professional journey that you are in.

Consequently, such training could also be relevant for organizations and their employees, in order to unleash the full potential of AI tools in workplace productivity but certainly also to develop people's ability to deal with this technology and the critical thinking skill set this requires.

Lastly, we have developed a white paper on how we generally intend to deal with generative AI at our business school. Learnings from this course have been included for inspiration on how our educators can integrate AI tools into their courses to foster critical thinking skills, applying the indirect approach mentioned above (Ennis, 1989) where such skills are taught on specific subject matter rather than focusing a course specifically on critical thinking.

References

Acar, O. A. (2023). Are Your Students Ready for AI? A 4-Step Framework to Prepare Learners for a ChatGPT World. *Harvard Business School Publishing*. [https://www.hbsp.harvard.edu/inspiring-minds/are-your-students-ready-for-ai].

Alsaleh, N. J. (2020). Teaching Critical Thinking Skills: Literature Review. *The Turkish Online Journal of Educational Technology*, **19**(1), 21-39.

Andreucci-Annunziata, P., Riedemann, A., Cortés, S., Mellado, A., del Río, M. T. & Vega-Muñoz, A. (2023). Conceptualizations and instructional strategies on critical thinking in higher education: A systematic review of systematic reviews. *Frontiers in Education*, **8**, 1141686.

Behar-Horenstein, L. S. & Niu, L. (2011). Teaching Critical Thinking Skills in Higher Education: A Review of The Literature. *Journal of College Teaching & Learning*, **8**(2), 25-42.

Calma, A., & Davies, M. (2021). Critical Thinking in Business Education: Current Outlook and Future Prospects. *Studies in Higher Education*, 46(11), 2279-95.

Daud, N. M. & Husin, Z. (2004). Developing critical thinking skills in computer-aided extended reading classes. *British Journal of Educational Technology*, **35**(4), 477-487.

Deo, S., Hinchcliff, M., Thai, N. T., Papakosmas, M., Chad, P., Heffernan, T., & Gibbons, B. (2023). Educating for the sustainable future: A conceptual process for mapping the United Nations sustainable development goals in marketing teaching using Bloom's taxonomy. *Journal of Marketing Education*, **0**(0), 1-13.

Ennis, R. H. (1989). Critical thinking and subject specificity: Clarification and needed research. *Educational Researcher*, **18**(3), 4-10.

Essien, A., Bukoye, O. T., O'Dea, X., & Kremantzis, M. (2024). The influence of AI text generators on critical thinking skills in UK business schools. *Studies in Higher Education*, **49**(5), 865-882.

Kirkpatrick, D. L., & Kirkpatrick., J. D. (2006). *Evaluating Training Programs. The Four Levels.* (3rd ed). New York: McGraw-Hill.

Lawrence, N., Serdikoff, S., Zinn, T., & Baker, S. (2008). Have we demystified critical thinking? In Dunn, D., Halonen, J., & Smith, R. (Eds.), *Teaching Critical Thinking in Psychology* (1st ed.). United Kingdom: Wiley-Blackwell.

Lipman, M. (1988). Critical thinking: What can it be? *Educational Leadership*, **46**(1), 38-43.

Mollick, E. R. & Mollick, L. (2023). Assigning AI: Seven Approaches for Students, with Prompts. *The Wharton School Research Paper*. [SSRN: https://ssrn.com/abstract=4475995].

O'Dea, X. C., & O'Dea, M. (2023). Is artificial intelligence really the next big thing in learning and teaching in higher education? A conceptual paper. *Journal of University Teaching and Learning Practice*, **20**(5), 1-17.

Spanjol, J., Rosa, A., Schirrmeister, E., Dahl, P., Domnik, D., Lindner, M., De La Cruz, M. & Kuhlmann, J. F. (2023). The potential of futures literacy for impact-oriented business schools. *Futures*, **146**, 103084.

Van Gelder, T. (2005). Teaching Critical Thinking: Some Lessons from Cognitive Science. *College Teaching*, **53**(1), 41-46.

Author Biography:

Sophie is also a professor for Marketing & Communication at Munich Business School (MBS), where she teaches behavioral marketing and consumer behavior. In 2022, she has been appointed Impact Officer and continues to develop the societal impact framework at MBS.

She is also the Senior Research Strategy Advisor at the European Food Information Council (EUFIC), a non-profit organization established in 1995 which stands up for science-based information on food and health. Among other things, she has been the Principal Coordinator of the EU FP7 funded project CLYMBOL – Role of health claims and symbols in consumer behavior.

She holds a PhD from the Munich School of Management at Ludwig-Maximilian-University, Munich. Her main area of research is consumer behavior and psychology, specifically decision-making regarding food, health and lifestyle.

Sophie Hieke

Sophie has published in numerous journals and held a position as Associate Editor for Public Health Nutrition from 2015 to 2019. She has won several prizes for her scientific publications, including the "Emerald Citation Award" in 2017 and "Best Paper of the Year" by the American Council of Consumer Interest in 2012. She also serves as a reviewer, key note speaker and is currently on the Expert Advisory Panel of Food Navigator.

Infographics as Research Tool - to Clarify ideas, for Categorization, Iterations, Reflections and as Interaction tool

Line Kolås, Oddlaug Marie Lindgaard and Ninni Anita Rotmo Olsen
Nord University, Norway
line.kolas@nord.no
oddlaug.m.lindgaard@nord.no
ninni.a.olsen@nord.no

Abstract: Higher education students learn to develop new knowledge through student research projects like bachelor's and master's projects. Based on introductory research methods courses, they learn to apply research methods during their projects, and, in a fast-paced world, using visualisations like infographics can be valuable. Infographics are visualisations that convey a message by presenting complex information quickly and clearly. Based on our previous teaching experience, students are skilled at collecting data but have difficulties with the analysis process of their research projects. The aim of this action research project was to examine the implications of using infographics as a teaching and learning method during student research projects. The innovation of our project is the use of infographics as a supplementary cross-disciplinary tool for analysis as opposed to its traditional use of merely presenting findings in students' research projects. Through several action research iterations, including planning, acting, observing, and reflecting, we have developed an innovative teaching method with a variety of workshop activities to help students analyse their data using infographics, for example through visual "elevator pitches", categorisations, visual models, illustrating the research process and consistency between research questions and findings. We found that key values of infographics as an analysis tool are clarification, categorisation, quality assurance, reflection, and interaction. The use of infographics leads to a more personalised understanding and an aesthetic perspective on the data and data analysis. The use of infographics enhances the students' reflections and is helpful in developing a holistic overview of their data and analysis. Our initiative shows that infographics, in combination with academic writing, have the potential to decode and activate meaning in a visual way and to create more distinct ideas.

Line Kolås, Oddlaug Marie Lindgaard and Ninni Anita Rotmo Olsen

1. Introduction

Based on experiences from both teaching a research methods course (MET1003 Research methods) for undergraduate students in their 5th semester and supervising the same students during their bachelor's project in the 6th semester, in addition to experiences with grading both bachelor's theses and master's thesis from our own university and other universities, there is a need to help students in the analysis phase of their student research projects. We experienced that the students are skilled at data collection, but that they struggle to analyse and present it in a sufficient manner, in some cases resulting in presenting raw data as findings or presenting many findings, without being able to see these in relation to each other. Our experiences relate to those of Cornford and Smithson (1996), who state that students often conduct data analysis in a weak manner. Hence the idea of trying to develop a teaching and analysis method which could address this problem and give students tools to improve the analysis process and the way they present their findings.

During the initial planning and exploring of the challenges the students had, we found that infographics are a versatile tool that can be used to improve student learning in a variety of educational contexts and could possibly be a fitting tool for us to teach the students.

1.1 The role of infographics in education

Naparin and Saad (2017) define infographics as "data visualizations that present complex information quickly and clearly, which includes signs, photos, maps, graphics, and charts. Infographics are visual representations that integrate information derived from data and graphics to convey a message." They are particularly well-suited for today's students who tend to have strong visual preferences (Jaleniauskiene & Kasperiuniene, 2023). While studying the different effects of infographics used as instructional tools for presenting complex information in higher education, Ibrahem and Alamro (2021) found indications that infographics are effective for improving students' achievement, e-learning and computer skills, and achievement motivation. According to Jaleniauskiene & Kasperiuniene (2023) infographics can be used in various educational contexts and can promote the development of critical thinking, information literacy, and visual literacy skills (Jaleniauskiene & Kasperiuniene, 2023).

1.2   Learning through creating infographics

Creating infographics is a student-active teaching approach that can be more beneficial for students than passively consuming teacher-made infographics. The process of creating infographics encourages students to think critically about information, select relevant content, and organise it in a visually appealing way (Jaleniauskiene & Kasperiuniene, 2023). This aligns with socio-cultural theories of learning, which emphasise the importance of collaboration and knowledge creation (Vygotskij et al., 1978). Seen with socio-cultural lenses, drawing can be regarded a cognitive and cultural tool, just as language, writing and counting (Dysthe, 2001).

1.3   Infographics and research-based learning

Infographics can also be a valuable tool in research-based learning environments. Visualising data can help students understand complex concepts and identify patterns (Krishnan et al., 2020; Tsujioka, 2018). Creating infographics based on their own research can further enhance students' learning and communication skills (Jaleniauskiene & Kasperiuniene, 2023).

2.   The infrastructure

2.1   Action research project

With the aim of improving practice, our interventions were based on an action research project (Elliot, 1991), where we first identified the problem and then ran several action research iterations, including planning, acting, observing, and reflecting. The interventions were done during the spring semesters of 2023 and 2024. Fig. 1 describes the details of our action research project.

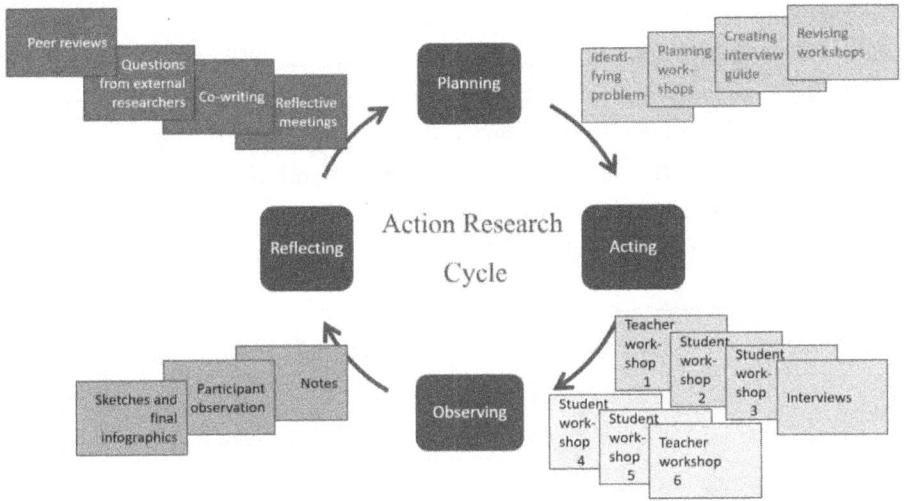

Figure 1 The details of the action research project that led to the proposed teaching method.

2.2 People

The students, who have taken part in the action research project, were third year bachelor students at an IT study program at a Norwegian university. The students have a research methods course (10 ECTS) in the fifth semester and are doing the bachelor's project (10 ECTS) in the sixth semester. The action research team consisted of a research methods teacher (who also yearly supervise some of the bachelor's projects), an art teacher (with expertise in visual perceptions) and a researcher/teacher from the university's competence centre within learning and technology. In addition, we hired an external expert in visual communication for initial three workshops (one for teachers / supervisors and two for students). The attendance of the workshops was voluntary.

2.3 Teaching method

The teaching method was developed through several iterations during the action research project where the problem statement was how infographics could be used in teaching or supervising student research projects (Kolås et al., 2023).

The teaching method consists of two workshops and a period in-between where the students work with their own student research projects. In the first workshop, they learn about visual communication including an activity working with mock data, and how to present and clarify findings through visual items, in addition to do some initial work on drawing symbols and icons related to their own research projects. After collecting their data, the second workshop focuses on activities where the students are working with their own data.

Figure 2 Student workflow when creating infographics.

During those two workshops, the students worked with nine different activities. Because Hsiao et al. (2019) suggest that students may benefit from first sketching their infographics using paper and pencil, we decided to focus on non-digital infographics in the workshops. The workshop activities included practical drawing activities focusing on different research phases and perspectives, based on their own student research project:

1. Elevator pitch – present your bachelor's/master's project with the use of few words, and then illustrate your elevator pitch! Use simple forms (circles, boxes, pyramids...)
2. Key words – Define three key words for your project and find icons to represent each key word.
3. Your process – Illustrate your research process: data collection, data analysis, findings, (conclusions).
4. Cluster your data – What are the similarities in your data? Cluster similarities and find a symbol for each cluster.

5. Make an overview – Take a bird's eye view of your codes/categories and find the 3-5 most important parts and illustrate the relations between them. Use boxes and arrows.
6. Consistency – Illustrate the relations between your research questions and your findings. Reflect upon whether your findings answer the research question.
7. Visual models – Illustrate your findings. What are the implications of your findings? Visual model of findings: complexity, parts vs the whole, connections/relations. What, how, why? To what degree does your infographics relate to your research question(-s)?
8. In-depth learning – Add relevant symbols to main topics in your literature review of the field. What relations can you find between own findings and the existing literature within the field?
9. Constructive feedback – Present your infographics/illustrations to two peer students. Give constructive feedback to each other.

During the workshops, the students got access to drawing equipment and a sketchbook. We touched upon the use of digital tools for the creation of infographics, but the exercises were paper-based. The student group knows software packages for visualisations and in their final bachelor's thesis, the students turned sketches from their analogue analysis process into digital infographics.

Line Kolås, Oddlaug Marie Lindgaard and Ninni Anita Rotmo Olsen

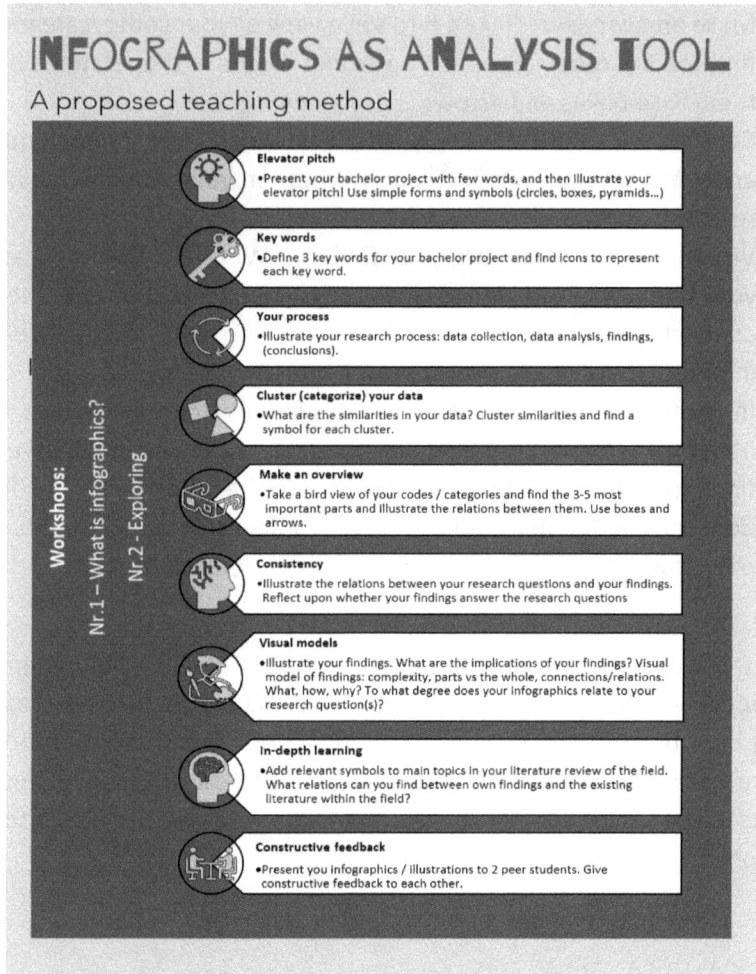

Figure 3 The proposed teaching method, including workshop activities for the use of infographics as an analysis tool.

2.4   More about the workshop activities

The initial workshop activity is an elevator pitch, which is added to help students obtain a clear understanding of their own project. This is useful to succeed with a project. It also teaches the students to use simple figures when illustrating. The second workshop activity focuses on finding and illustrating key words for their projects, where the idea is to show the students the difference between simple figures and icons. These key icons are valuable to clarify their understanding of the main parts of their projects. The "your process" workshop activity will help students understand the difference between main phases of a research project, e.g. data collection, data analysis, discussion etc. The students should also visualize the details of each phase, e.g. how they collect data, types of data, preparations before data collection etc. It also emphasizes that the students must become aware of what analysis method they are planning to use and how to report this in their thesis. The "Cluster your data" workshop activity was included, even though categorization is not necessarily an analysis technique used in all research projects. There is, however, often useful to do some kind of clustering of data. This workshop activity will help the clustering / categorization process, using illustrations. The following activity focuses on the relations between codes and categories and highlights the importance of weighting which parts are more important than others, but also to help students realize that there might be connections between categories that should be highlighted. This activity also trains students in using simple illustrations like boxes and arrows. The "Consistency"-activity will help students to illustrate the importance of the relationship between their research questions and their findings. Students sometimes forget that there must be consistency throughout their projects, as they find new and interesting areas throughout their project, and hence their projects will appear as fragmented. In the activity called "Visual models," students are asked to illustrate their findings. Through iterations, visual models of early findings may prove to be valuable in the analysis process. Illustrations will potentially make it easier to see complexity, parts vs the whole, how well it relates to their research question etc. In the "In-depth learning"-activity, the students are asked to illustrate the relationship between own findings and the existing literature in the field to illuminate the connections and to help students write the final report/thesis, where it is expected that the students can see these connections. The last activity, the "Constructive feedback", is an important activity. The students show their illustrations to peers and get feedback on their illustrations/infographics convey the correct message, and what is unclear about their infographics. This feedback often leads to improvement of their infographics.

The nine workshop activities can be altered to suit the student group. It is not necessary to use all the activities, and sometimes it is necessary to adjust some of the activities. In addition, the facilitator can alter the order of the activities. If the students mainly work with quantitative data, an additional workshop activity can be to learn to simplify and elucidate diagrams etc. Here, the visual communication field can offer helpful resources.

2.5   Examples of students' infographics
Below we have added some examples of the students' infographics, illustrating several of the phases of their infographic development. During the process of creating their infographics, they started with pencils and paper and ended up creating infographics using digital drawing tools and graphic software. The hand drawn examples were initial sketches during the first workshop, while the digital versions were published in their bachelor's theses.

Image 1 Early example of student doodling 1

Image 2 Early example of student doodling 2

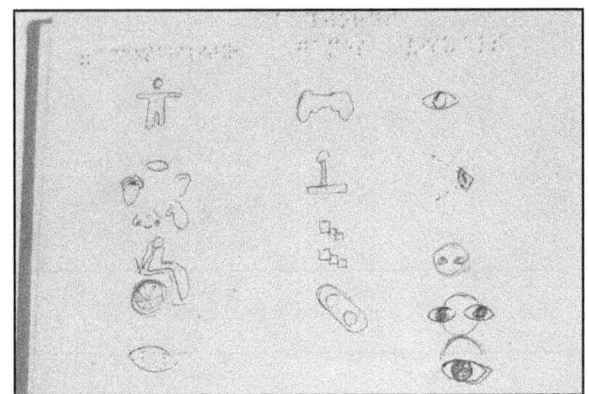

Image 3 Early example of student doodling -exploration of different versions

Image 4 Student doodling.

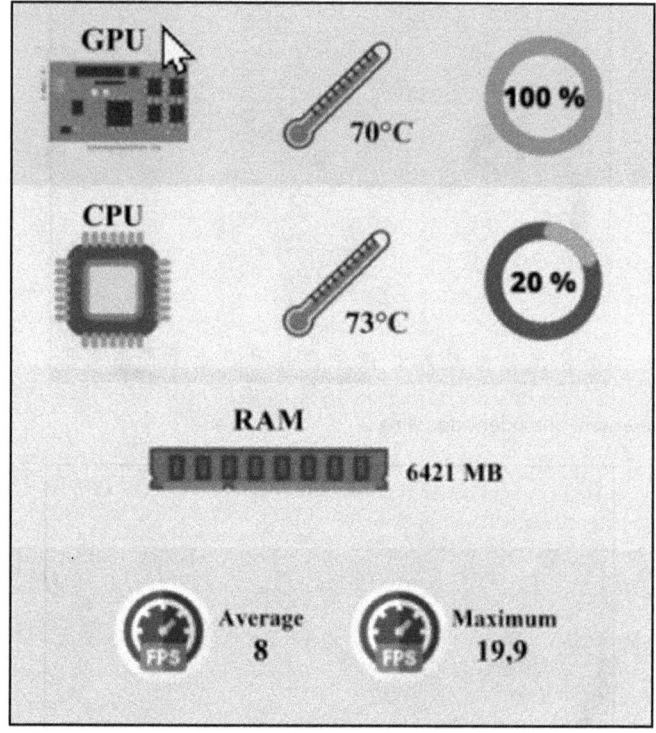

Image 5 Screenshot of student infographic used in final thesis.

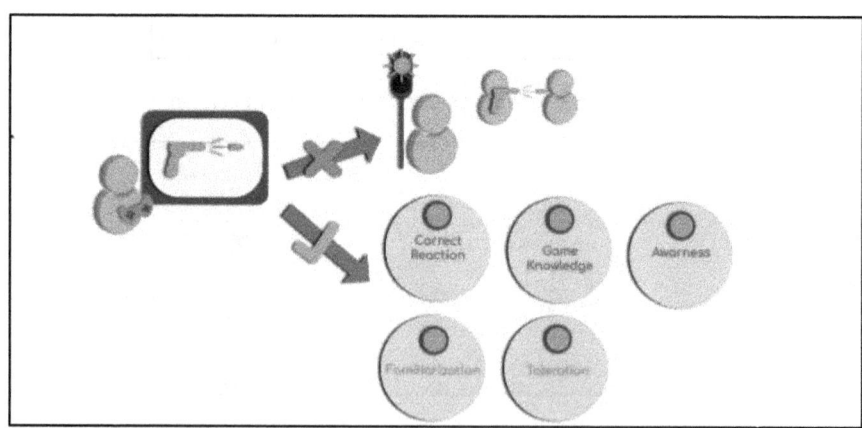

Image 6 Screenshot of student infographics used in final thesis.

3. The challenges

The use of infographics in the analysis phase of a research project was unknown territory when the project started. The teaching staff had to seek knowledge and research about the use of infographics. A lot of the existing literature were upon research done of students producing posters, and the use of posters created by students. There was a gap in the research literature about solutions of helping students with their research projects using infographics as an analysis tool. There was also a need to investigate theory about visual communication. Our proposed teaching method contributes to the existing field with innovative ideas regarding the use of infographics as an analysis tool, not merely as a presentation tool of the final results. As an analysis tool, infographics can give different and useful perspectives on the analyses of the research data and the overall project.

Since this was a cross-disciplinary project that is not connected to a specific course, there were challenges toward getting hold of students to attend and be a part of the research project. The option to make students attend the workshops, and to participate in interviews, were limited, as the attendance at the workshops were voluntary. Hence fewer students than hoped for, did attend. During the first year of the project, the project group reached out to potential teachers and invited to a teacher workshop prior to the two student workshops. Some teachers attended this workshop, but since this is a somewhat unknow approach to teach students analysis, they expressed some scepticism and feared that introducing the visual aspects of data analysis would confuse the students when they worked with their student research projects. We have therefore throughout the process learned that we need to address not only the students, but also the teachers / supervisors. The second year of running the workshops we also invited the teachers to attend the workshops. It is also necessary to clarify towards both teachers and students that the use of infographics in the analysis phase is not a substitute for traditional analysis methods, rather a supplement. Students taking part in the workshops report that the visual approach to data analysis is a valuable supplement.

4. How the initiative was received by the students

The overall feedback from the attending students was positive. They appreciated the workshops and the possibility to use visual elements both when doing analyses and when presenting their findings.

In the following, quotes gathered from the students through observations and interviews are presented structured by the main outcomes from our research:

Use of workshops as the teaching design: One student's response regarding how the workshops influenced the learning process was as follows: *"That was definitely what was most fun this semester. To actually experience something different than just sitting alone writing. That gets boring and the motivation is a bit like 'meh' ... But the workshops – the ones who joined them and the ones who I have talked to, we all thought that we learned a lot and that it was good use of our time."*

We were also surprised that one student actually needed a confirmation, that infographics are allowed also in a thesis, which s/he expected to be very text-based. *"I was thinking about using some kind of infographics for my thesis before the workshop. But I was not sure if I could. If I was allowed to do it. And in what way and to what extent I could use them."*

Clarification of ideas: One of the participating students described the experience: *"It helped me to have a clearer view of what I found. And it gave me the opportunity to present my interpretations of the findings in a way that I found very supportive."*

Categorisation: One student did not realize that s/he was using infographics as part of the analysis, mainly because the research theory concepts were new. S/he first claimed that s/he only used infographics to present findings, but later described how infographics were used to categorize the data: *"I'm not very good at writing, so for me it's really helpful when I can sit and draw different things and be able to categorize that way...before I made them (categories) into words... I chose to first use figures as categories, before I made a list of category names."*

Line Kolås, Oddlaug Marie Lindgaard and Ninni Anita Rotmo Olsen

Working in iterations: Because translating ideas into a graphical format is a process, several iterations of the infographic may be necessary before it is finalized (Hsiao et al., 2019). As supervisors, we observed that the student-generated infographics were closely connected to the raw data in the first iteration. One student concluded that *"It's a very good idea to use infographics in the first stages / early stage of the research"* and that *"it is a very powerful tool. Even in the early stages of the research."* The student later categorized, interpreted, and refined the data through several iterations with feedback, which lead to a further understanding of what analysis is, before the final version was presented.

Regarding their work on icons, one student reported that s/he made many versions: *"there were 6-7 different versions. I felt it necessary."*

Reflections: In our suggested workshop activities, reflections are related to different phases of the research process, including the infographics' relations to research questions, the infographics' relations to findings, the research questions' relations to findings, and the findings' relations to existing literature. To ensure consistency in the research project and in-depth learning through the understanding of concepts, methods, and content relations, in addition to meta-reflections, such as the following from one of the students: *A key factor related to the use of infographics in a bachelor's project is to have data that is good enough. Without data it is impossible to get anything good out of this – then you have to try to get something out of nothing, and that is impossible."*

Infographics as interaction tool: An important part of the workshops was to share sketches and discuss with peers and teachers how to use visualizations in their student research projects, and they described in the interviews how they also continue to use the infographics as an interaction tool after the workshops. One student described how they used peers in the iterative process of creating visuals: *"I showed them what I had created so far and asked them what they thought it expressed. I got different answers, and I realized that I had to make changes. I further described what I wanted to communicate and asked if they could suggest icons that would work better."*

5. The learning outcomes

The proposed teaching method acts as scaffolding in the students' learning process and fosters awareness and directs attention to the critical analysis phase of the research process. It is not supposed to be a substitute to traditional analysis methods but is valuable as a supplement in both quantitative and qualitative data analysis. The workshops are social arenas with focus on active learning, where students engage in practical, hands-on tasks. As facilitators of the workshops, the teachers address Damsgaard's (2019) key elements for the transitions of students' learning: student activity, mastering, structure and relationships with peers and teachers.

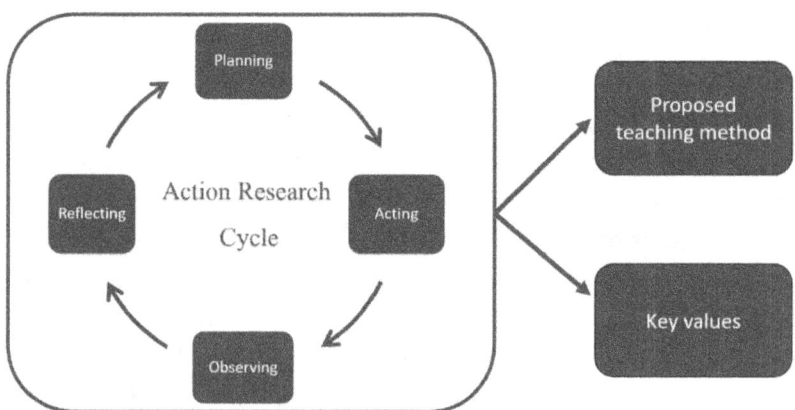

Figure 4 The action research cycle and the outcomes.

5.1 Key values of using infographics as an analysis tool

We found the following key values of using infographics as an analysis tool:

- Infographics as a tool for clarifying ideas: Using symbols, icons and other graphical representations of their data, students were able to see connections / relations and to get an overview of their project.
- Infographics are useful for categorisation: Using graphical representations, the students analysed the data with a different approach than previously learned and were able to use infographics as a tool to categorize / cluster.

- Infographics in iterations: Working with visual representations of data, categories, initial findings etc. made the students do many iterations / versions, and through this work the students were able to dig deeper into their data and do a thorough analysis.
- Infographics for reflections: Through some of the workshop activities, students used infographics for reflections of their own project and learning process. The visualizations concretize problem statement, data, findings, and other important parts of a student research project.
- Infographics as interaction tool: The graphical work of the students made it easier for the students at an early stage to share, discuss and evaluate their analysis and initial findings.

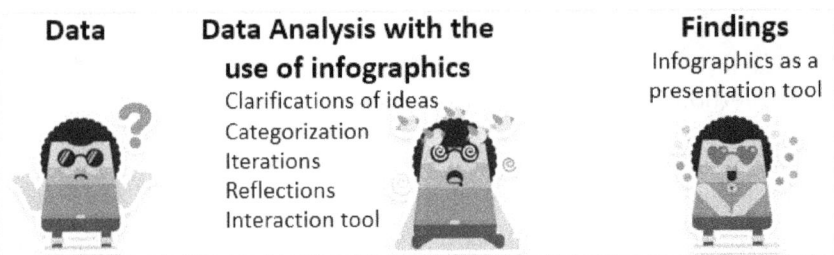

Figure 5 Overview of three main phases of a student research project and the key values of infographics in the analysis phase.

5.2 How the outcomes were evaluated

The outcomes were evaluated through several iterations in the action research project, e.g. by the students both through evaluations of each workshop and more in-depth statements given during the interviews. In addition, we examined the use of infographics in the students' final reports/theses. We also received feedback and questions from external researchers after presenting the project at several seminars for other researchers who also received funding from Excited, the Centre for Excellent IT Education. Our initial research paper (Kolås et al., 2023) was peer reviewed and we have read and incorporated the feedback.

The proposed teaching method has been evaluated by peers during and after each teacher workshop, and we have been able to revise the content, type of activities and usefulness of the proposed teaching method through the iterations of our action research project.

6. Plans to further develop the initiative

In the future, the initiative will be further developed through additional iterations of planning, acting, observing and reflection. Also, during the spring semester of 2024, we offered a second round of the workshops to bachelor students working on their bachelor projects. We will collect data about their experiences and opinions among the students after they finish their bachelor's project also this study year. There are plans for trying out and evaluating this method also to master's students, to other study programs, as well as to teachers/supervisors at Nord University, since this is a cross-disciplinary teaching method.

To expand the teaching method beyond bachelor students in our program, we need to actively promote it among university colleagues, internally and externally. Increasing awareness is crucial, so we plan to write a news article for the university intranet and give talks and run workshops about the methodology in different fora, highlighting the teacher workshops and encouraging participation.

There are also plans to further research the effects of the method as we continue to use the method among our students.

References

Cornford, T., & Smithson, S. (1996). Analyzing research data. In (pp. 108-135). London: Macmillan Education UK. https://doi.org/10.1007/978-1-349-13863-0_7

Damsgaard, H. (2019). *Studielivskvalitet*. Scandinavian University Press (Universitetsforlaget).

Dysthe, O. (2001). *Dialog, samspel og læring*. Abstrakt forl.

Elliot, J. (1991). *Action research for educational change*. McGraw-Hill Education (UK).

Hsiao, P. Y., Laquatra, I., Johnson, R. M., & Smolic, C. E. (2019). Using Infographics to Teach the Evidence Analysis Process to Senior Undergraduate Students. *J Acad Nutr Diet, 119*(1), 26,30-29,30. https://doi.org/10.1016/j.jand.2017.10.022

Ibrahem, U. M., & Alamro, A. R. (2021). Effects of Infographics on Developing Computer Knowledge, Skills and Achievement Motivation among Hail University Students. *International Journal of Instruction*(1), 907-926.

Jaleniauskiene, E., & Kasperiuniene, J. (2023). Infographics in higher education: A scoping review. *E-Learning and Digital Media, 20*(2), 191-206.

Kolås, L., Lindgaard, O. M., & Olsen, N. A. R. (2023). Infographics as an Analysis tool in Student Research. *NIKT: Norsk IKT-konferanse for forskning og utdanning*. https://www.ntnu.no/ojs/index.php/nikt/article/view/5709

Krishnan, J., Maamuujav, U., & Collins, P. (2020). Multiple utilities of infographics in undergraduate students' process-based writing. *Writing & Pedagogy, 12*(2–3), 369-394.

Naparin, H., & Saad, A. B. (2017). Infographics in education: Review on infographics design. *The International Journal of Multimedia & Its Applications (IJMA), 9*(4), 5.

Tsujioka, K. (2018). A case study of ICT used by big data processing in education: discuss on visualization of RE research paper. Proceedings of the 6th International Conference on Information and Education Technology,

Vygotskij, L. S., Cole, M., John-Steiner, V., Scribner, S., & Souberman, E. (1978). *Mind in society : the development of higher psychological processes*. Harvard University Press.

Author Biographies

Line Kolås is an Associate Professor at Nord University, Norway – also awarded the title "Excellent Teaching Practitioner". She has a PhD in informatics, and her research interests are e-learning systems, ICT in education and IT didactics. She is currently a researcher and cluster leader in Excited – Centre for Excellent IT education, focusing on pedagogical practices.

Oddlaug Marie Lindgaard is a senior adviser/lecturer at Nord University. She has an MBA in Educational Leadership, and her research interests are digital teaching, flexible learning, pedagogy, and change management. She is currently a researcher and lecturer at the Centre for Learning and Technology.

Ninni Anita Rotmo Olsen teaches Arts and Crafts within the Faculty of Education and Arts, and CG Art Animation within the Faculty of Social Sciences at Nord university. Her pedagogical practices are characterized by their performative nature, while her research focuses on the intersections of art-based inquiry and sustainability in education.

Empowering Future Generations: Integrating Haptic Learning and Sustainability into University Education for Enhanced Engagement and Resilience

Klaus Kuehnel [1] and Manuel Au-Yong-Oliveira [2,*]
[1]PhD Student of DBI Program, University of AveiroPortugal
[2]INESC TEC - Institute for Systems and Computer Engineering, Technology and Science; GOVCOPP - The Research Unit on Governance, Competitiveness and Public Policies; DEGEIT - Department of Economics, Management, Industrial Engineering and Tourism, University of Aveiro, Portugal
*Correspondence: mao@ua.pt
klaus.kuehnel@hotmail.com

Abstract: This research delineates an innovative educational framework poised to transform university pedagogy from traditional lecture-based teaching to a more dynamic, hands-on, and sustainable approach (Dixit et al., 2024; Hixson et al., 2018), by a university lecturer doing a PhD at the University of Aveiro and who has quickly taken on an innovative stance in academia, spurred on by his PhD supervisor. At the heart of this educational overhaul is the emphasis on fostering deep, meaningful learning experiences over mere knowledge transmission, with a strong focus on cultivating students' critical thinking skills. Through active engagement in questioning, analyzing, and synthesizing information, this model promotes a culture of inquiry and reflection, essential for intellectual growth. Structured Literature Research (SLR) is highlighted as a key instrument for deepening students' connection to their studies, enhancing personal expression, and emotional engagement. The framework also seeks to balance traditional academic values with an emphasis on individualism, encouraging students to pursue paths aligned with their personal and academic goals. This includes developing adaptability and 'grit' to navigate changing societal and professional landscapes (Gunnarsson, 2020). Educators are identified as pivotal to the successful implementation of this reform, with a call for collaborative efforts among faculty to adopt and champion these innovative educational practices. This collective endeavor aims to equip students with the skills and mindset necessary for making substantive contributions to their fields. In summary, the article articulates a compelling vision for reimagining higher education to address contemporary challenges, advocating for a holistic model that emphasizes cognitive and personal growth (Soubhari et al., 2023). This approach sets a foundation for students to tackle future challenges with confidence and creativity, representing a significant shift in higher education philosophy towards a more engaging, reflective, and adaptable learning environment (Sotelo, 2024).

Keywords: scientific thinking, critical thinking, teaching resources, skepticism, education policy

1. Introduction

In today's evolving educational landscape, updating teaching strategies is crucial (Maipita et al., 2023). This concept introduces an innovative way to enhance university lectures by creating a tactile and sustainable learning environment (Albers et al., 2024). Moving beyond traditional, theory-heavy lectures, it emphasizes hands-on, haptic learning and sustainable practices to make education more engaging and relevant (Romanova & Anisimova, 2023). This approach not only aids in grasping complex concepts but also develops students' practical skills and creativity, while emphasizing the importance of sustainability in learning materials and long-term application (Björkman et al., 2022). The goal is to equip students for the modern world's challenges, transforming them into well-rounded individuals who can contribute positively to their fields. Research indicates a need for such pedagogical innovations, as current literature on higher education lacks discussions on adapting cross-disciplinary synergies (Rodríguez-Izquierdo, 2022) (figure 1). This initiative aims to reevaluate and enhance teaching methods by integrating tactile learning, critical thinking, and individualism, addressing the evolving demands and pressures faced by students today (Burge, 2008). The University of Aveiro, where the first author is doing his PhD, being a young and entrepreneurial university, highly approves of innovative teaching methods, to capture the attention – hearts and minds – of students.

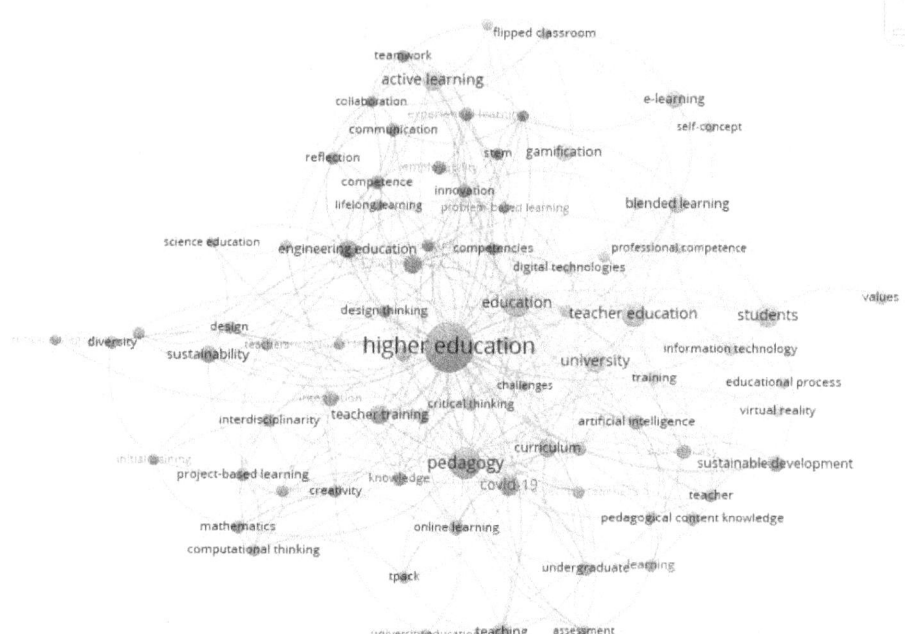

Figure 1: VOSviewer for SCOPUS search - university AND pedagogical AND concept

The structured literature research has made evident a gap in academia, as regards universities and the higher education process (Hixson et al., 2018). The existence of integrated internships is good and placing an additional emphasis on active learning (including the flipped classroom and collaboration) and will lead to the betterment of teaching in higher education institutions (please see figure 2). Albeit the case study method and intense involvement that engages are also competences that are still not mainstream enough in the lecture theatre, in certain countries. Diversity and inclusivity (regarding student backgrounds and learning styles) as well as the curriculum as a tool have not yet become the main focus, despite the rise of artificial intelligence which will, no doubt, like most other areas of society, end up having a tremendous effect on day-to-day life in higher education (Green, 2022; Martin & O'Meara, 2019).

Klaus Kuehnel and Manuel Au-Yong-Oliveira

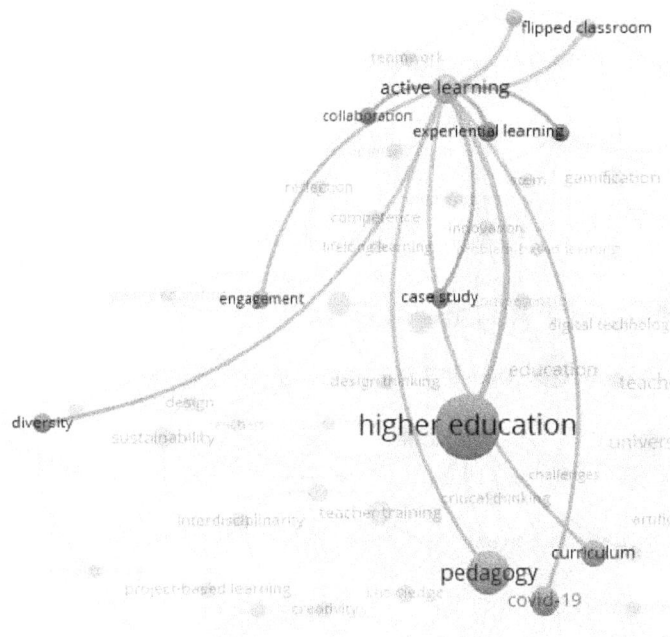

Figure 2: VOSviewer detail - Connections to the focus concept of active learning

2. Background

As a lecturer, the first author developed and agreed the basic concept with the authorized committees of the university and evaluated it neutrally according to the criteria of statistical recording of opinions within the student body. The following questions were asked of a total of 895 students in various departments according to a predetermined distribution key. The voluntary and neutral nature of the survey was guaranteed at all times. The evaluation was carried out by independent, audited professors who certified the legality and quality of the survey. In the following, the general catalogue of questions is narrowed down to a student number of 208 by personalizing the lecturer. This made it possible to analyze the results of each lecturer in comparison with his or her colleagues in other areas. However, the focus was not on comparing lecturers but on the interdisciplinary, practice-orientated approach. Here is the catalogue of questions and the resulting findings. The initiators of the questions were well aware that this data is not representative due to the small number of respondents and the fact that it was only carried out at one university. However, the basic approach and the nature of the questions provide a very good insight into the methodology itself, as well as the adjustment of the methodological sub-components (Daniels et al., 2023).

The Catalogue of questions to evaluate the pedagogical methods of the lecturer Klaus Kühnel in Department 07 - Business Informatics - Subject "Digital Transformation" (Moore et al., 2023)

2.1.1 INTRODUCTION TO THE LESSON

- ow did you find the first lesson with Mr. Kühnel?
- What differences did you notice compared to other teachers?

2.1.2 TEACHING METHODS

- How did Mr. Kühnel convey his lecture (e.g., lectures, discussions, practical exercises)?
- Which of Mr. Kühnel's methods did you like best and why?
- How did Mr. Kühnel's teaching differ from traditional teaching methods?

2.1.3 STUDENT INTERACTION

- How did Mr. Kühnel involve you and your classmates in the lessons?
- Did you feel that your opinion and ideas were valued by Mr. Kühnel in class?
- How did Mr. Kühnel influence the semester group and the cohesion among the students?

2.1.4 PERSONAL DEVELOPMENT

- To what extent has Mr. Kühnel influenced your view of life and your goals?

- What new interests or passions have you discovered through Mr. Kühnel's teaching?
- Has Mr. Kühnel helped you to gain more confidence in your own abilities? If so, how?

2.1.5 Critical Thinking and Creativity

- How did Mr. Kühnel encourage your ability to think critically and find creative solutions?
- Were there specific tasks or projects that particularly challenged your critical thinking or creativity?

2.1.6 Motivation and Inspiration

- How did Mr. Kühnel influence your motivation and enthusiasm for learning?
- What quotes or statements from Mr. Kühnel have particularly inspired you and why?

2.1.7 Long-term Effects

- How do you think Mr. Kühnel's teaching methods will influence your future educational and professional career?
- Which of Mr. Kühnel's lectures or exercises will you use in your future life?

2.1.8 Criticism and Suggestions for Improvement

- Are there any aspects of Mr. Kühnel's lecture that you found less positive?
- What suggestions would you have to further improve Mr. Kühnel's lecture?

2.1.9 COMPARISON WITH OTHER TEACHERS

- How would you rate Mr. Kühnel compared to your other teachers?
- Which aspects of Mr. Kühnel's teaching methods would you like to see in other lecturers?

2.1.10 OVERALL SATISFACTION

- On a scale of 1 (not satisfied) - 10 (completely satisfied), how satisfied are you overall with Mr. Kühnel's teaching?
- Would you recommend Mr. Kühnel as a lecturer? Why or why not?

This list of questions is intended to help students reflect on their experiences and impressions of Mr. Kühnel's teaching methods in a structured way and give a well-founded assessment.

3. The evaluation and findings

The evaluation of teacher Mr. Kühnel by the students of the school according to the questionnaire follows below (Almujadidi et al., 2022). The following evaluation by two independent lecturers at the same university resulted in the following result:

3.1 Introduction to the lecture

The students found the start of the first lecture with Mr. Kühnel refreshing and unconventional. Many were surprised and at the same time enthusiastic about his method of taking the students out of their usual ways of thinking, for example by reading the poem "Carpe Diem".

3.2 Lecture Methods

Mr. Kühnel conveyed his lessons mainly through discussions, practical exercises and inspiring lectures. His unconventional methods, such as standing on the tables to gain a new perspective, were particularly popular. The students appreciated this variety and the opportunity to actively participate in the lecture instead of just passively listening.

3.3 Student Interaction

Mr. Kühnel actively involved all students in the lecture and encouraged the expression of opinion. He created a climate of mutual respect and appreciation. The students felt encouraged to express their own ideas and thoughts freely, which led to a positive dynamic and strong cohesion in the class.

3.4 Personal development

Many students reported that Mr. Kühnel had a lasting influence on their view of life and their goals. They felt inspired to pursue their own passions and make bold decisions. Through the lecture, some students discovered new interests, especially in the field of literature and poetry.

3.5 Critical thinking and creativity

Mr. Kühnel encouraged students' critical thinking and creativity through tasks that challenged them to think outside the box and develop their own points of view. Examples such as writing and reciting one's own poems or analyzing literary works in an unconventional way were particularly appreciated.

3.6 Motivation and inspiration

The students' motivation and enthusiasm for learning increased noticeably, and Mr. Kühnel inspired them with his passion and motivational speeches. Quotes such as "Carpe Diem" and his invitation to live life to the fullest left a deep impression and were often highlighted as particularly inspiring.

3.7 Long-term effects

The students agreed that Mr. Kühnel's lecture methods will have a positive influence on their future educational and professional careers. Many stated that they would like to apply Mr. Kühnel's lessons in their future lives. They felt encouraged to think independently and go their own ways.

3.8 Criticism and suggestions for improvement

Some students found that Mr. Kühnel's methods were too unconventional and therefore sometimes confusing for some fellow students. It was noted that a better balance between traditional and unconventional lectures could be helpful. Suggestions for improvement mainly concerned the integration of more structured elements to facilitate the transition to the new methods.

3.9 Comparison with other teachers

Compared to other teachers, Mr. Kühnel was rated predominantly positively. His passion and commitment were particularly highlighted. Many students wished that other teachers would use similar methods to make the lectures more interesting and inspiring.

3.10 Overall satisfaction

The general satisfaction with Mr. Kühnel's lecture was very high. The students felt well looked after and inspired. The majority would recommend Mr. Kühnel as a teacher, as he knew how to motivate and promote them in a unique way.

Mr. Klaus Kühnel

at Hochschule München
in SS 2023 by 78 students, with each bar representing a different category of evaluation.

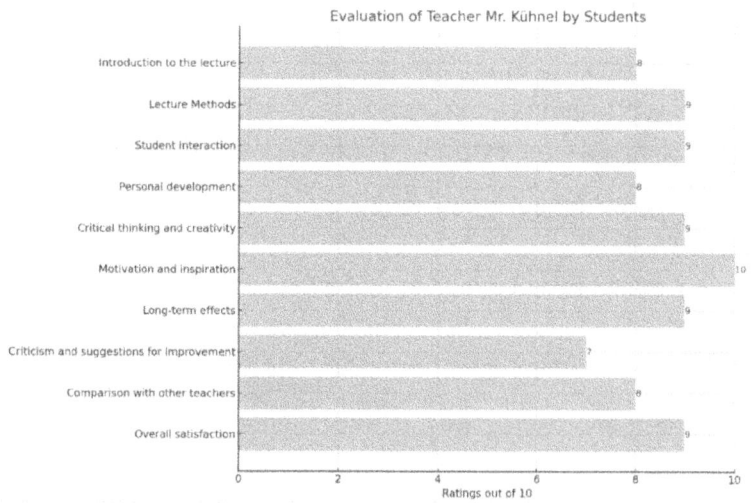

Figure 3: A classification of Klaus Kuehnel as a lecturer

Figure 4: Teacher Klaus Kuehnel – unconventional methods in the classroom

Summary: The review shows that Mr. Kühnel is appreciated by the students of the boarding school as an exceptional teacher who has left a lasting impression through his unconventional methods and inspiring personality. Most of the students felt positively changed by his lecture and motivated to reach their full potential. Please see figures 3 and 4.

4. General considerations of the individual points (Rossum et al., 2020)

4.1 Promoting independence and critical thinking

The current socio-political issue that due to the manipulative development of the media, especially internet-based platforms, critical thinking and independence are becoming increasingly central and thus complement traditional educational methods (Daniels et al., 2023). These skills enable students to critically evaluate information, recognize bias and formulate reasoned arguments. Only well-informed people therefore also acquire the important independent skills that are necessary for academic success and participation in the labor market. Crucial to this is the emphasis on evidence-based strategies that critically address cognitive biases and logical fallacies, to address development and thus make a meaningful contribution to society (Luig et al., 2018).

## 4.2	Structured Literature Research (SLR) in University Education

A methodological approach to improve the formation of opinions and the necessary background knowledge, as well as to learn academic writing and critical reading of scientific papers, it is crucial to work systematically and according to established rules. This enables students to navigate and evaluate the enormous wealth of digital and virtual content. Structured literature research (SLR) is the best way for students to open up this path and engage intensively with literature, thereby improving their expression and analysis skills (Watrianthos et al., 2023). This significantly improves academic literacy. SLR plays a crucial role in the training of qualified researchers and the development of information literacy (Albers et al., 2024).

## 4.3	Tension between individualism and collectivism

The tension between the pure transmission of facts and the enrichment of knowledge in various methods of selecting and evaluating these is a skill that needs to be taught to students (Harris et al., 2023). This characteristic is constantly exposed to the tension between individual perspectives and the empathic ability to put oneself in the shoes of other cultures and ways of thinking. Under these cornerstones, it is a challenge but also a change to develop critical analyses and systematic syntheses from the multitude of information sources offered (Daniels et al., 2023). Teaching students the skills to analyze and creatively synthesize new perspectives on issues is therefore of paramount importance. In addition, the ability to work in a team and empathize with the immediate or intended target group is an essential basis for any acceptance of the resulting educational effectiveness (Kelley et al., 2007).

4.4 Method for sustainable self-help

Another very important characteristic is dealing with conflicts. A process that has become known as the GRIT method, after the American psychologist Charles Osgood, to de-escalate bitter and seemingly hopeless conflicts and prepare for a negotiation, is characterized by passion and perseverance in the pursuit of long-term goals (Romanova & Anisimova, 2023). Intrinsic motivation and long-term aspirations, academic achievement, self-efficacy and emotional engagement are very important for success in order to encourage students to take on challenges and realize their full potential as they progress through higher education (Daniels et al., 2023).

4.5 Introduction to the Specific Objectives of the Initiative

The primary goal of our initiative is to revolutionize university education by fostering a tactile and sustainable learning environment that departs from the traditional lecture-focused model (Brown, 2006). Our approach emphasizes haptic learning methods, sustainable practices, and long-term knowledge retention. We aim to engage students more actively in the learning process, equipping them with practical skills and critical thinking capabilities necessary for navigating the challenges of an ever-changing world (Rodríguez-Izquierdo, 2022).

4.6 Survey: Analysis of Mediating Effects of Interdisciplinary Identity

The influence of the interdisciplinary teaching system on the interdisciplinary competence of engineering students was analyzed by means of a targeted survey of students who were taught using this teaching method and examined using correlation and significance tests (Kim, 2023). The application of design thinking in the development and implementation of an interdisciplinary curriculum was the basis for this. The study, which was conducted from March to December 2022 at the Munich University of Applied Sciences in the field of business informatics, included field observations, in-depth interviews and document analyses to understand the associated challenges and strategies. Summarizing the key findings - The haptic transfer of knowledge is one of the key tenets of this successful study. To enhance students' collaboration and co-creation skills, design thinking was used in interdisciplinary curriculum design and was found to be effective, with an emphasis on practical application and integration. The use of visual tools, communication techniques and on-site observations are crucial for teaching. Design thinking cycles (empathizing, defining, ideating, prototyping, testing) were used in projects to teach and practice interdisciplinary skills. Not everything went according to plan, however; the challenges encountered were the difficulties of integrating different cognitive and ideational aspects from different areas. Communication problems due to the heterogeneous background of the students was one of the reasons for this. As in the past, the lecturer played a leading role and emphasized the importance of professional growth and reflection. Thus, students are encouraged to engage in real-world problem solving to improve their practical and theoretical understanding. Deeper insights into the challenges of interdisciplinary teaching in a post-pandemic context were provided by the study and emphasized the need for adaptation and deepening of learning outcomes (Watrianthos et al., 2023). A key advantage is the independent development of knowledge content based on practical tasks. The confrontation with topics from everyday life in the lecturer's practice is therefore a very interesting basis for the students. Encouraging the students to work out solutions in the first step using the means available to them up to this point ensures that the subject matter is penetrated first. Using the right methodology is not important in this case. After the initial presentation of the problem and the associated content, the framework for the basic topic is provided. It is not the solution-orientated approach that is the aim of this knowledge transfer model, but rather a reflection on the actual task that forms the basis for sustainable learning (Ashrafi-rizi et al., 2023). Working in a team brings with it a very differentiated view of the subject matter with the various socialization perspectives, which corresponds to the character of interdisciplinary knowledge transfer. The rudimentary approach of Design Thinking is a practicable method for offering an interdisciplinary curriculum design with practical strategies for overcoming challenges in teaching. The importance of integrating real-world applications and fostering a collaborative learning environment and the lessons learnt support the development of effective interdisciplinary educational practices (Wanieck et al., 2020).

5. Practical example: Improving engineering education outreach in rural counties through engineering risk analysis

Student surveys were analyzed to gauge interest in science, technology, engineering and mathematics (STEM) (Albers et al., 2024). There were no significant differences between the aptitude scores of applicants from rural and urban counties. It was notable that the number of freshmen from rural areas was lower relative to urban areas. The consequence was the introduction of a practical engineering course, which was organized on the university's own initiative in cooperation with a number of grammar schools in the districts around Munich. A technical risk study was carried out at 5 of the 35 grammar schools. Derived from the international "Smart-City-Project", a real technical infrastructure and a natural hazard phenomenon (flooding) were constructed, which makes the direct hazard potential tangible and illustrates visible effects on the life of the district in order to convey the social value of STEM subjects to the students . A series of pre- and post-tests monitored the significance of the results to determine the effectiveness of the hands-on teaching methods and engineering risk analysis of a real-world infrastructure. The tests showed a very positive impact on students' perceptions of STEM subjects in the pursuit of engineering innovation. The use of a real water risk analysis of a nearby infrastructure as a motivational tool in rural high schools was thus very effective and raised awareness of STEM subjects as a foundation for engineering. This study underpinned the effectiveness of haptic, real-world experiential teaching methods.

6. The Infrastructure

6.1 People

6.1.1 *Support Staff to Facilitate the Integration of New Teaching Methods and Technologies.*

Critical to the success of this pedagogical shift is a dedicated team of support staff who work behind the scenes to ensure the seamless integration of new teaching methods and technologies into the classroom (Rossum et al., 2020).

This team includes instructional designers, technology specialists, and administrative personnel who collaborate closely with educators to develop, test, and refine innovative teaching and learning solutions. Instructional designers assist educators in creating engaging and effective learning materials that align with the initiative's goals. They focus on the design and delivery of curriculum content that is both accessible and challenging, ensuring that learning experiences are well-structured and comprehensive (Martin & O'Meara, 2019). Technology specialists provide the necessary technical expertise to support the use of new tools and platforms within the learning environment. They are responsible for setting up virtual reality setups, managing learning management systems, and ensuring that all technological resources are up-to-date and functioning optimally. Their work enables educators to incorporate a variety of digital and interactive tools into their teaching, further enriching the learning experience for students (Watrianthos et al., 2023). Together, educators and support staff form the backbone of the initiative's infrastructure, working collaboratively to transform the educational landscape. Their efforts are aimed at not just revolutionizing how knowledge is delivered and absorbed but also at preparing a new generation of learners to thrive in an ever-changing world. Through their dedication and expertise, they strive to create a learning environment where students are not only intellectually stimulated but also empowered to make a positive impact in their fields and beyond (Goemaes et al., 2020).

6.2   Systems

A Learning Management System (LMS) Tailored to Support Haptic and Sustainable Learning Methodologies (Soubhari et al., 2023). The initiative uses a specialized Learning Management System (LMS) designed for haptic and sustainable learning, integrating tools and resources for interactive, experiential education. Key features include haptic learning tools, sustainability resources, collaborative workspaces, and personalized learning paths (Aghnatios et al., 2021). The system uses evaluation systems like NASA-TLX to assess and improve the teaching and learning process, focusing on cognitive load, mental and physical demand, temporal demand, performance, effort, and frustration level. These measures help adapt teaching strategies and content to student needs, ensuring a responsive and evolving educational environment. This approach aims to offer a dynamic, engaging learning experience that emphasizes hands-on participation and environmental sustainability (Eliyas et al., 2017).

7. The Challenges

This research identifies challenges and strategies within an educational reform initiative, focusing on overcoming initial resistance to novel pedagogical approaches and integrating sustainability into the curriculum.

7.1 Challenge 1: Resistance to New Pedagogical Methods

Initial resistance among faculty and students accustomed to traditional educational methodologies was a significant barrier. This resistance was rooted in reluctance to alter established routines and skepticism regarding the efficacy of innovative teaching strategies (Silocchi et al., 2021).

7.1.1 Strategies for Overcoming Resistance:

Educational Workshops: To mitigate resistance, workshops were conducted to elucidate the benefits and mechanics of new educational approaches, featuring hands-on demonstrations and testimonials from early adopters (Van Dormael et al., 2007).

Pilot Programs: Selected faculty and students participated in pilot programs, experiencing the benefits of innovative methods firsthand. Success stories from these pilots were disseminated widely to foster trust and support (Chouvarda et al., 2019).

Continuous Support: Support structures were established, providing training, resources, and a feedback mechanism to facilitate the transition to new pedagogical strategies (Teodorowski et al., 2019).

7.2 Challenge 2: Integration of Sustainable Practices into the Curriculum

The incorporation of sustainability into educational programs necessitated a thorough overhaul of course content, resources, and instructional methods to reflect sustainability principles (Long et al., 2020).

7.2.1 Strategies for Integrating Sustainability

Curriculum Review and Revamp: A task force reviewed the curriculum to integrate sustainable practices, updating course materials and including sustainability case studies within project-based learning tasks.

Sustainability Training for Educators: Teachers were trained in sustainability concepts and methodologies to effectively weave these principles into their instruction.

Resource Development: New educational materials focusing on sustainability were created to support the revised curriculum.

7.3 Challenge 3: Adapting to Diverse Student Engagement and Feedback

Variations in student engagement levels and feedback diversity posed challenges in tailoring the learning experience to meet all students' needs effectively (Minteer et al., 2023).

7.3.1 Strategies for Addressing Engagement and Feedback Diversity

Tailored instructional approaches and feedback mechanisms were developed to accommodate different engagement levels and feedback types, ensuring a responsive and inclusive learning environment. Through these targeted strategies, the initiative aimed to address resistance, foster an inclusive and sustainable educational framework, and adapt to the varied needs of the student body, thereby enhancing the overall learning experience (Silocchi et al., 2021).

7.4 Reception by Users or Participants:

This research evaluates the impact of a novel educational framework aimed at enhancing student engagement, critical thinking, and knowledge application through dynamic, hands-on learning experiences. The initiative, well-received by the majority of students for its interactive approach, also saw educators reporting improvements in student creativity and engagement. Continuous feedback has been pivotal for refining teaching methods to align with student needs (Björkman et al., 2022).

8. Plans to Further Develop the Initiative

Expansion of the initiative intends to include more disciplines and faculties, adapting the approach to suit different fields of study. Further integration of technology will be achieved to enhance haptic and interactive learning experiences. Continuous evaluation and refinement of teaching methods based on student performance data and feedback will occur. Development of partnerships with other educational institutions and industries to provide students with real-world learning opportunities will take place. This restructured outline provides a comprehensive overview of the initiative, highlighting the specific objectives, the infrastructure in place to support these goals, the challenges encountered and how they were addressed, the positive reception from users, the learning outcomes achieved, and plans for future development.

9. Conclusion

As a best practice, the learning objectives, the learning topic, the resources at hand, as well as the needs of the individual learners, will dictate what teaching method we choose to use. The best scenario may be to use a certain mix of teaching methods to then realize what we can hope to achieve. Learning outcomes may be visualized vis-à-vis a combination of teaching methods. Our study discusses how a tactile, secure, and sustainable learning environment may positively impact higher education quite innovatively. Centuries-old more traditional lecture theatre methods need to be questioned and haptic experiences as well as long term memorization and retention need to be the approach aimed for including the promotion of critical thinking to improve student independence and individuality. How indeed may a Structured Literature Research (SLR) play a role of central importance for personal and emotional development? The SLR needs to be the emphasis according to one's passion and goals in life and "grit" and resistance will have an increasing effect on all sorts of expected success rates, including both in academia and in the professional marketplace. We have sought to emphasize the need to be more flexible amidst the continuous flux and change we have witnessed as technology has taken over in many aspects of life. Despite the uncertainty involved students must have specific goals to which academia may contribute more fully. Innovative teaching methods are necessary - such as the NASA-TLX (Task Load Index) - to monitor learning and modify where necessary certain teaching methods to meet student needs. At the end of the day, education needs to center itself on what matters - the student – adapting teaching approaches to a whole new technological environment where passive learning will no longer achieve the desired outcomes in a whole new world of disruption and with no one knowing what we will need to know in five years' time to survive and flourish and achieve the quality of life or previous generations.

Acknowledgements

This work was financially supported by the Research Unit on Governance, Competitiveness and Public Policies (UIDB/04058/2020) + (UIDP/04058/2020), funded by national funds through FCT - Fundação para a Ciência e a Tecnologia.

References

Aghnatios, M., Darloy, T., Dictor, J., Gasparovicova, M., Drouot, C., Gasperini, F., & Bouchez, T. (2021). Advanced practice nursing: representations of actors in this new model [Article]. *Sante Publique, 33*(4), 547-558. https://doi.org/10.3917/spub.214.0547

Albers, M. M., Reitsma, M. M., Benning, K. K., Gobbens, R. J. J. R., Timmermans, O. A. A. M. J. O., & Nies, H. L. G. R. H. (2024). Developing a theory of change model for a learning and innovation network: A qualitative study [Article]. *Nurse Education in Practice, 77*, Article 103954. https://doi.org/10.1016/j.nepr.2024.103954

Almujadidi, B., Adams, A., Alquaiz, A., Van Gurp, G., Schuster, T., & Andermann, A. (2022). Exploring social determinants of health in a Saudi Arabian primary health care setting: the need for a multidisciplinary approach [Article]. *International Journal for Equity in Health, 21*(1), Article 24. https://doi.org/10.1186/s12939-022-01627-2

Ashrafi-rizi, H., Samouei, R., Mohammad Reza, S., & Yamani, N. (2023). Identifying the challenges of holding comprehensive exams in the Ph.D. programs of Iranian medical universities: A protocol for qualitative research [Article]. *Journal of Education and Health Promotion*, *12*(1), Article 293. https://doi.org/10.4103/jehp.jehp_111_23

Björkman, I., Feldthusen, C., Forsgren, E., Jonnergård, A., Lindström Kjellberg, I., Wallengren Gustafsson, C., & Lundberg, M. (2022). Person-centred care on the move - an interview study with programme directors in Swedish higher education [Article]. *BMC Medical Education*, *22*(1), 589. https://doi.org/10.1186/s12909-022-03657-4

Brown, S. J. (2006). The experiences of lecturer practitioners in clinical practice [Article]. *Nurse Education Today*, *26*(7), 601-608. https://doi.org/10.1016/j.nedt.2006.01.016

Burge, L. (2008). 'Crafting the future': Pioneer lessons and concerns for today [Article]. *Distance Education*, *29*(1), 5-17. https://doi.org/10.1080/01587910802004811

Chouvarda, I., Mountford, N., Trajkovik, V., Loncar-Turukalo, T., & Cusack, T. (2019). Leveraging interdisciplinary education toward securing the future of connected health research in Europe: Qualitative study [Article]. *Journal of Medical Internet Research*, *21*(11), Article e14020. https://doi.org/10.2196/14020

Daniels, S., Bartholomew, E., & Chambliss, H. (2023). Development of the Together - Teens&20s microsite, an online resource for adolescent and young adult cancer patients [Article]. *PEC Innovation*, *3*, Article 100235. https://doi.org/10.1016/j.pecinn.2023.100235

Dixit, A. C., Harshavardhan, B., Ashok, B. C., Sriraj, M. A., & Prakasha, K. N. (2024). Innovative Pedagogical Approaches for Diverse Learning Styles and Student-Centric Learning [Article]. *Journal of Engineering Education Transformations*, *37*(Special Issue 2), 178-188. https://doi.org/10.16920/jeet/2024/v37is2/24039

Eliyas, S., Briggs, P., & Gallagher, J. E. (2017). The experience of dentists who gained enhanced skills in endodontics within a novel pilot training programme [Article]. *British Dental Journal*, *222*(4), 269-275. https://doi.org/10.1038/sj.bdj.2017.172

Goemaes, R., Beeckman, D., Verhaeghe, S., & Van Hecke, A. (2020). Sustaining the quality of midwifery practice in Belgium: Challenges and opportunities for advanced midwife practitioners [Article]. *Midwifery*, *89*, Article 102792. https://doi.org/10.1016/j.midw.2020.102792

Green, C. (2022). Consequences of neoliberal traits in curriculum design; English influences and the implementation of moral education in schools in the United Arab Emirates [Article]. *Globalisation, Societies and Education*, *20*(5), 669-681. https://doi.org/10.1080/14767724.2021.1993150

Gunnarsson, G. J. (2020). What About Transformative Religious Education? In *Religious Education in a Post-Secular Age: Case Studies from Europe* (pp. 83-97). Springer International Publishing. https://doi.org/10.1007/978-3-030-47503-1_5

Harris, A. H. S., Finlay, A. K., Hagedorn, H. J., Manfredi, L., Jones, G., Kamal, R. N., Sears, E. D., Hawn, M., Eisenberg, D., Pershing, S., & Mudumbai, S. (2023). Identifying Strategies to Reduce Low-Value

Preoperative Testing for Low-Risk Procedures: a Qualitative Study of Facilities with High or Recently Improved Levels of Testing [Article]. *Journal of General Internal Medicine*, *38*(14), 3209-3215. https://doi.org/10.1007/s11606-023-08287-0

Hixson, C., Ingram, E. L., McCord, R., & Williams, J. M. (2018). Lean LaunchPad and customer discovery as a form of qualitative research. ASEE Annual Conference and Exposition, Conference Proceedings,

Kelley, F. J., Kopac, C. A., & Rosselli, J. (2007). Advanced Health Assessment in Nurse Practitioner Programs: Follow-Up Study [Article]. *Journal of Professional Nursing*, *23*(3), 137-143. https://doi.org/10.1016/j.profnurs.2006.12.005

Kim, E. (2023). Sustainable New Product Development for Ten Thousand Villages, a Fair-Trade Social Enterprise: Empowering Women and Economic Development through Problem-Based Service Learning [Article]. *Sustainability (Switzerland)*, *15*(8), Article 6452. https://doi.org/10.3390/su15086452

Long, J. A., Jowsey, T., Henderson, K., Merry, A. F., & Weller, J. M. (2020). Sustaining multidisciplinary team training in New Zealand hospitals: A qualitative study of a national simulationbased initiative [Article]. *New Zealand Medical Journal*, *133*(1516), 10-21. https://www.scopus.com/inward/record.uri?eid=2-s2.0-85086354881&partnerID=40&md5=633708c3624100d41d48befb5217ba0a

Luig, T., Asselin, J., Sharma, A. M., & Campbell-Scherer, D. L. (2018). Understanding implementation of complex interventions in primary care teams [Article]. *Journal of the American Board of Family Medicine*, *31*(3), 431-444. https://doi.org/10.3122/jabfm.2018.03.170273

Maipita, I., Dongoran, F. R., Syah, D. H., & Sagala, G. H. (2023). TPACK, ORGANIZATIONAL SUPPORT, AND TECHNOSTRESS IN EXPLAINING TEACHER PERFORMANCE DURING FULLY ONLINE LEARNING [Article]. *Journal of Information Technology Education: Research*, *22*, 41-70. https://doi.org/10.28945/5069

Martin, A. C., & O'Meara, P. (2019). Perspectives from the frontline of two North American community paramedicine programs: An observational, ethnographic study [Article]. *Rural and Remote Health*, *19*(1), Article 4888. https://doi.org/10.22605/RRH4888

Minteer, S. A., Cheville, A., Tesch, N., Griffin, J. M., Austin, J. D., Mitchell, S., Leppin, A. L., & Ridgeway, J. L. (2023). Implementing cancer symptom management interventions utilizing patient-reported outcomes: a pre-implementation evaluation of barriers and facilitators [Article]. *Supportive Care in Cancer*, *31*(12), Article 697. https://doi.org/10.1007/s00520-023-08114-6

Moore, K., Sanchez-Pena, M. L., Chen, Q., McAlister, A. M., Burris, C., & Mowatt, J. V. (2023). Integrating Participatory Methods in the Study of Equity and Inclusion. ASEE Annual Conference and Exposition, Conference Proceedings,

Rodríguez-Izquierdo, R. M. (2022). *Service Learning at a Glance* [Book]. Nova Science Publishers, Inc. https://doi.org/10.52305/HTYC7259

Romanova, O. A., & Anisimova, K. V. (2023). Demonstration Exam in Continuing Entrepreneurial Education within the VET1 and HE2 Systems [Article]. *Vysshee Obrazovanie v Rossii*, *32*(6), 54-75. https://doi.org/10.31992/0869-3617-2023-32-6-54-75

Rossum, K., Finlay, J., McCormick, M., Desjarlais, A., Vorster, H., Fontaine, G., Talson, M., Ferreira Da Silva, P., Soroka, K. V., Sass, R., James, M., Tong, A., Harris, C., Melnyk, Y., Sood, M. M., Pannu, N., Suri, R. S., Tennankore, K., Thompson, S., . . . Bohm, C. (2020). A Mixed Method Investigation to Determine Priorities for Improving Information, Interaction, and Individualization of Care Among Individuals on In-center Hemodialysis: The Triple I Study [Article]. *Canadian Journal of Kidney Health and Disease, 7*. https://doi.org/10.1177/2054358120953284

Silocchi, C., Junges, J. R., Moehleck, V., & Diercks, M. S. (2021). Institutionalization of care practices for chronic conditions and the management of assistance in Primary Health Care* [Article]. *Interface: Communication, Health, Education, 25*, Article e200506. https://doi.org/10.1590/interface.200506

Sotelo, H. (2024). Employing Critical Organic Writing for the Truth About Speaking of Critical Race Theory in the Classroom: My Narrative [Article]. *Journal of Latinos and Education*. https://doi.org/10.1080/15348431.2024.2318328

Soubhari, T., Nanda, S. S., & Shah, M. A. (2023). Is new wine in a new bottle? Re-engineering poverty architecture through the Finnish model of education in India. In *Fostering Sustainable Businesses in Emerging Economies: The Impact of Technology* (pp. 167-186). Emerald Group Publishing Ltd. https://doi.org/10.1108/978-1-80455-640-520231011

Teodorowski, P., Cable, C., Kilburn, S., & Kennedy, C. (2019). Enacting evidence-based practice: Pathways for community nurses [Article]. *British Journal of Community Nursing, 24*(8), 370-376. https://doi.org/10.12968/bjcn.2019.24.8.370

Van Dormael, M., Dugas, S., & Diarra, S. (2007). North-South exchange and professional development: Experience from Mali and France [Article]. *Family Practice, 24*(2), 102-107. https://doi.org/10.1093/fampra/cml070

Wanieck, K., Ritzinger, D., Zollfrank, C., & Jacobs, S. (2020). Biomimetics: teaching the tools of the trade [Article]. *FEBS Open Bio, 10*(11), 2250-2267. https://doi.org/10.1002/2211-5463.12963

Watrianthos, R., Ahmad, S. T., & Muskhir, M. (2023). Charting the Growth and Structure of Early ChatGPT-Education Research: A Bibliometric Study [Article]. *Journal of Information Technology Education: Innovations in Practice, 22*, 235-253. https://doi.org/10.28945/5221

Author Biographies

Klaus Kuehnel; Graduate engineer in electrical engineering. Coach in industrial implementation of process / change management in USA, Germany, China. Lecturer at University of Munich – Academic supervisor at Bachelor / Master's level. Supervisor for startups. Consultant for industrial projects – SixSigma MasterBlackBelt. Doctoral candidate in Business Innovation. Authoring a book with Springer.

Manuel Au-Yong-Oliveira; On 1st march 2023 Manuel (PhD - FEUP, 2012; Habilitation – University of Aveiro, 2022) was awarded an honourable mention by the University of Aveiro for his research in the social sciences at the University of Aveiro Annual Researcher Awards ceremony. Manuel previously worked in industry in the management consultancy, health, book publishing, advertising, water treatment and metallurgic (gas cylinders) sectors.

Making Philosophy Relevant to Process and Practice: Exploring Rich Data through Assessment Journeys

Stephen Linstead
University of York, UK
stephen.linstead@york.ac.uk

1. Introduction to the Specific Objectives of Teaching the Initiative

This initiative is based on a compulsory doctoral course on the Philosophy and Process of Management Research in the School for Business and Society, University of York. Students' areas of specialisation are extremely diverse, from mathematical finance to narrative studies of identity. Our ESRC Doctoral Training Partnership expects students to participate in a shared social science conversation, developing understanding with other disciplines, and focusing on wider social challenges.

This terrain of the processes of inquiry, applying to all disciplines from identifying problems to devising methods from theory to practice without imposing a particular paradigm, hasn't been mapped. Burrell and Morgan's (1979) seminal contribution remains a valuable baseline. What was needed was a flexible framework that kept different elements of the research process in balance, whatever the paradigm, demystifying ontology, epistemology, methodology, axiology, praxeology and cosmology. Students should to recognise, by the type of questions they are asking and addressing, whereabouts in the research process they are currently located - what "-ology" they are exercising - without being bewildered by the terminology. They should be able to distinguish between multi-, inter-, and transdisciplinarity, and translate between different disciplines.

Stephen Linstead

1.1 Background and the Model 2002-17

From 2002-17, I developed such a roadmap, christened the "research diamond", which has been used successfully in 200 theses, in the UK, Australia, France, Hong Kong, Netherlands, and Thailand. This was used with individuals, rather than being the basis of a course. PPMR developed from this in 2014 varying from 12 to 20 students. In 2017 I introduced a new form of assessment to act as a learning vehicle, embedded within the diamond model rather than simply a terminal mode of examination, to fully integrate the elements of the course, motivating students to put their knowledge to use by applying philosophical concepts to interpreting rich data with multidisciplinary elements both qualitative and qualitative. I used recent full-length ethnographies with organisationally relevant content for analysis. These books were engaging, passionate, moving, addressing real and complex problems. I wanted the assessment vehicle to take them on a *journey* making students feel as well as think. In what follows I expand on the "diamond" model, how the assessment works, and discuss some of the "journeys" taken with it.

1.2 The Underlying Question

"How do I state my epistemology or ontology stances..." is an actual and common, question from students being taught social science and particularly business and management research methods in the 21st century. Much has changed for the better in the past 40 years for this to be commonly posed. But there is a downside. The 1980s phenomenon of paradigm incommensurability gave rise to the 1990s' "paradigm wars". It wasn't enough to *know* the paradigms, students were often expected to *commit* to a paradigm explicitly. At times this became obsessive. As Burrell and Morgan (1979) had shown, there was considerable heterogeneity within each paradigm. Halfpenny (1982) went further identifying 12 types of positivism alone. Blaikie (1993; 2007) emphasised 4 research strategies - deduction, induction, abduction and retroduction. This represents 2 more options than were commonly taught in research texts until quite recently.

But on the downside Blaikie also came up with a blizzard of *10 research paradigms* (positivism, critical rationalism, classical hermeneutics, interpretivism, critical theory, ethnomethodology, social realism, contemporary hermeneutics, structuration theory, feminism); *6 ontologies* ('shallow realist', 'conceptual realist', 'cautious realist', 'depth realist', 'idealist', and 'subtle realist'); and 6 epistemologies ('empiricism', 'rationalism', 'falsificationism', 'neo-realism', 'constructionism', and 'conventionalism') to complicate matters further. Despite its comprehensiveness, there are significant omissions in this list, yet 7 types of realism are present: Simon Lodge, reviewing it, suggested that this went beyond idiosyncracy towards a systematic rewriting of intellectual history.

This bewildering problem of what I have called "ismism" (Linstead 2004) means that disparate but related tendencies become categorised as homogenous. The paradigm - the "ism" - then becomes a mechan-ism *sui generis*. All paradigms suffer as a result. Common tabulations of paradigms and their features deliver an inevitably static picture of the dynamics of research in which they frequently caricature their object. Diagnostic tools developed from such problematic categorisations may do as much harm as good. I sought in this project to develop a tool that would help students to navigate the confusing and contradictory paradigm forest by focusing on the research process, showing how different types of philosophical question feature at different stages of the research journey - utilising "ologies" rather than "isms". I also teach particular perspectives through *people* (ie philosophers through their stories) rather than from *positions*; through *processes* (ie what they did) rather than *paradigms* (I populate the structured spaces with story and narrative).

Bergson argued for a contextually relational transdisciplinary plurality, rather than the competitive pluralism of a market for ideas: philosophy needed to *adapt its methods to whatever reality it found itself facing,* with ideas morphing to fit the problems encountered. It's not a matter of underlying beliefs and assumptions enforming thought styles and paradigms - although addressing these is a good place to start - it involves much more. Tsang (2017) claims to have written the only book on the philosophy of management research, and despite its merits, it ignores the paradigm approach, which is usually a sign of commitment to implicitly universalising a single paradigm. He begins by asserting that "the field of management research is commonly regarded as or aspires to be a science discipline" and accordingly focuses on explanation, assumptions, theory testing, generalization, replication, and a realist view of historiography. The assertion is false: management *science* and the philosophy of *science* take this view, but management is also an *art*, and philosophy itself is one of the *humanities*. Both perspectives have relevance - just like light can be a wave and a particle.

More general research textbooks face an insuperable challenge - how to convey the importance of being able to think philosophically without oversimplifying; falling into the trap of overcategorizing or typologizing; creating false dichotomies by which to distinguish between nuanced approaches; or committing Ryle's category errors. Here we encounter false equivalences in which some approaches operating at different levels are elevated to the plane of a "philosophy"; yet other categories are overstuffed with the work of several major philosophers being crammed into a holdall category such as postmodernism. Even in the very best of such overview works, this inevitably falls short. In many texts some individuals and approaches who don't fit categories disappear. Rather than understanding categories, and tidying research into them, it's the much messier passage of ideas and the processes of their crystallisation, translation and dissolution that, I will try to embrace. Philosophy here is creative and dynamic, not mechanical, and it is improvised - producing newness not novelty.

1.3 Looking at Process – The Research Diamond

Watching the US TV series *Law and Order* I was struck by one of the lieutenants who lectured a young uniformed policeman saying "We don't make assumptions, we're detectives". It was like watching a rerun of the previous term with my students. "We draw your attention to assumptions" I hear myself saying "so you don't have to make them without knowing that you are doing so, and maybe you don't have to make them at all". The terms "beliefs, values and assumptions" are widely misunderstood as being the same thing - varieties of ontology. But beliefs are primarily meontology, values are axiology, and assumptions are an unreflexive common sense version of ontology or cosmology. Narrative ethnographer H.L. Goodall Jr, who blended philosophy with storytelling seamlessly, saw himself as an organizational detective carefully looking for clues with an open mind. Too often when students feel they need to choose or worse, sign up to a paradigm, they close down what they have just opened up and the voyage of discovery never gets out of harbour. I wanted to give them a tool to help them become philosophical detectives, able to combine science and serendipity.

The model (Fig. 1) is neither cyclical nor input-output process based. The journey can begin from any entry point. For example, researchers with data analytic skills in population ecology and investment in expensive bespoke software, will be looking to research opportunities where they can use this and will enter the model via the method. Most of us will enter by looking at the Problem, which in the first instance is the "presenting" Problem, refined through the literature review. In our applied field of inquiry the problem has two dimensions - the extent to which it is a problem for *scholarship*, and the extent to which it is a problem for *practice*, the former being most significant. Once we have determined the problem, we tease out what *kind* of a problem it is and scrutinise this through the ontological concepts of the literature review. This is the *Ontological Question* which involves asking "What is the nature of the research problem and its setting? What kind of problem is it? Is it stable or changing? Should I emphasise order or change, being or becoming, structure or process? And what sort of theory fits this sort of problem?"

A PhD is a conceptual story about decisions and choices made, and how they were justified. Here we begin to insert the basic paradigmatic framework (interpretive, functionalist, radical structuralist, radical humanist), exploring approaches that may lie beyond it: critical, postpositivist, post paradigm, postmodern, practice and process approaches. These thread their way between the ontological questions around the nature of the problem into the *Epistemological Question* – "What is known about the problem? What are the areas of agreement, conflict and controversy? What *needs* to be known about the problem? Where are the gaps? What kind of knowledge is entailed to develop further understanding, and what kind of knowledge can we generate?"

Depending on what kind of knowledge we need to generate to address identified gaps, we begin our research design by addressing the *Methodological Question* - What methods are necessary to access the type(s) of knowledge required by the problem? Or what type of problem does our methodological knowledge and expertise require, and does *this* problem fit what *we* can bring to it. If not, can we acquire that knowledge and skill? This prevents false knowledge claims - where approaches geared towards understanding claim to have "tested" or "proved" something, while approaches aimed at narrower causality claim to know what this means to a community

Figure 1: A model of research process- the Research Diamond

Turning back towards the research problem, we also now consider whether our method keeps us in touch with the complex realities of the field problem. Laboratory studies often explain behaviour under controlled conditions very well but fall apart under field dynamics. "Do the methods applied - eg the questions asked - still relate to the original problem posed? Have we followed the clues to the mystery but mislaid the body?"

Moving from method to the wider problem context, we encounter the *Praxeological Question* which confronts issues of practice, process, and communities of practice – access, sample availability, resources, ethics (a consideration everywhere in the process but specifically here), client contact/relationships, intervention/application issues, sectoral features and consultancy styles. These are important for pragmatist and practice-based thinking and how method may need to be improvised or customised. Here we look at the mutual effects of the organization on the conduct of the project, and the project on the organization. This where *reflexivity* comes to the fore. We also need to consider the *Political Question*, which connects the problem to the wider organizational context, and power – "Who owns the research problem? What do they want us to do? Who else has a stake in it? Who might want to stop us doing it the way we want to, or at all? Who has a legitimate voice in it? Who is going to get something out of it or be affected by it?"

Finally, the outer context, beyond the organization, activates the *Axiological Question*. What values and ideas shape and arrange the overall project, the type of impact it seeks to have, and the contribution it wishes to make. Ethics again is central. Here the researcher asks, reflexively, "how will my contribution be *consumed*? How does it relate to current *ideas* and debates available in the public intellectual field? How does it relate to current broader *social concerns*, including ideological ones? What will be *my position* relative to these and my broader contribution? Where is my *intellectual support*? Who are my role models? What ultimately are the *values and principles* that sustain my research – what is *axiomatic* for me?"

The course itself, rather than take up a position of paradigm incommensurability or agonistics, or one that requires students to choose or declare a commitment to a paradigm, uses the paradigm approach to *describe typical research journeys* around the diamond.

2. The 2017-2024 Initiative

When I introduced the new form of assessment to motivate students to put their knowledge to use by applying philosophical concepts to interpreting rich data, with multidisciplinary elements both qualitative and qualitative, by what criteria did I select the assessment texts? The ideal text is a full-length ethnography written for wider audience by an author who is an academic and has supporting high quality academic work. It should be a compelling and enjoyable read that is moving – that has emotional reality or *affect*. The topic should be challenging and significant, and the questions addressed should have social, organizational, and personal significance. The inquiry should be carried through with conceptual rigour and may also be contested or controversial. It should present a rich, complex inner and outer

context, by combining different primary and secondary sources, qualitative and quantitative. Ideally it should have won or been nominated for awards/recognition. The texts used in the initiative were:

Table 1: Sources used in Course Assessment

Year of use	Author	Year	Title	Publisher
2017	Karen Ho	2009	Liquidated: An Ethnography of Wall Street	Durham NC: Duke University Press
2018	Timothy Pachirat	2011	Every Twelve Seconds: Industrialized Slaughter and the Politics of Sight	New Haven, CN: Yale University Press
2019	Alice Goffman	2014	On the Run: Fugitive Life in an American City	Chicago IL: University of Chicago Press
2020-21	Kimberley Kay Hoang	2015	Dealing in Desire: Asian Ascendancy, Western Decline, and the Hidden Currencies of Global Sex Work	Oakland CA: University of California Press
022	Matthew Desmond	2016	Evicted: Profit and Power in the American City	New York NY: Penguin
2023	Mark de Rond	2017	Doctors at War: Life and Death in a Field Hospital	Ithaca NY: Cornell University Press
2024	Katherine Sobering	2022	The People's Hotel: Working for Justice in Argentina.	Durham NC: Duke University Press

I wanted, above all, to provide a rich data source, which was complex but engaging, humanly moving as well as intellectually challenging, that featured conscientious social science and excellence in storytelling, with personal, organizational and wider significance and philosophical/ethical/reflexive depth. The author should be an academic, having supporting high quality academic work with current relevance, writing for wider audience than just academics and creating a compelling and enjoyable read. Awards and good reviews were a bonus.

They should be multidisciplinary with data presentations that provide rich, complex context, inner and outer, combining different primary and secondary sources, qualitative and quantitative, with multiple paradigm analytic potential. Their topic should be challenging and significant - even exciting - exploring questions with conceptual rigour even if arguments were contested or controversial. Finally they should be moving, with emotional reality delivering affect, that would potentially change their ways of seeing, and the reader would happily re-read for pleasure.

Ho worked in a Wall Street broker and uncovered the connections between the historical development of neoliberalism and globalisation and the everyday expendability of people in a financialised economy. She demonstrated how hegemony did not just depend on being 'smart' - even with degrees from Stanford and Princeton, she found they were in the wrong subjects and carried the wrong social and cultural capital. Pachirat worked in slaughterhouse, on the floor and in quality management, and showed how the everyday dynamics of shutting out the unacceptable underpinnjngs of everyday consumption constitutes a 'politics of sight' that underpins international relations in violence based social strategies. Goffman spent time working alongside and socialising with black gang members in Philadelphia, encountering racism, criminality, victimisation and ordinary people trying to survive - and how various institutions from health to housing to the penal system compound the problems they are set up to solve. Hoang worked in various administrative roles and at different levels in the sex industry in Ho Chi Min City. In the process she looked at how the industry is shaped by masculinities, race, speed of economic expansion, risk, and East-West shifts in the balance of power. Desmond worked with and studies tenants, landlords and the homeless in Baltimore in deprived communities showing how simple exploitative models do not match reality, linking personal stories to public policy. De Rond took considerable risks in supporting a team of field surgeons in Afghanistan, where astonishing levels of performance were maintained in the most traumatic of circumstances, confronting huge existential questions and developing institutional theory around team conflict. Sobering worked in a hotel that was saved from shutdown when the Argentine economy collapsed by becoming a worker-owned cooperative. She explores the impact of the changes in relations this entailed between workers, managers, different types of customers, legalities, markets, and local-international dynamics as they fought for survival over a decade.

A typical *assignment setting* instructs students to first read for pleasure, all the way through. They are guided to follow and *feel* the whole journey and remember that the field of social inquiry can involve both the sciences and the humanities. They should then review class materials on paradigms, post paradigm and beyond paradigm approaches, critical, postmodern and process philosophical approaches. They should take care not to *review* the book but read the additional articles to get a full sense of its dimensions and potential. Then they should use the book as a *rich data source* approaching it from the Research Diamond perspective, systematically asking the appropriate questions. They may identify a different research problem to the one the book focuses on – as long as they fully develop it.

Then they should review the familiar paradigm, multi-paradigm and postparadigm approaches covered in class remembering to distinguish between paradigmatic variety and multi-, inter-, and trans- disciplinary approaches in their thinking. They can then *either* analyse the text through one or more of these lenses, or if they identify a *new* problem, show how they would select one of these approaches to research it. Finally, they must take a *reflexive* position and a) consider how taking this approach might provide new opportunities for researching this topic in this setting; and b) consider how what they have discovered through this exercise might augment or transform their understanding of *their own research practice* in their PhD.

3. The infrastructure

The initiative required little in the way infrastructure to support it, that wasn't already available via our institutional library and IT systems. of resources except time, imagination and hard work. From 2002 I was involved in organizing research training in my own institutions and internationally and began to deliver the model as part of flexible workshops. It was a small course and although it required some breadth to teach it, the shortage of expertise in one person if I was not available was a constraint. In 2014 it was incorporated into the new course for the Doctoral Training Centre. The structure needed to change to a more conventional format to suit full-time students over a semester, and integrate with existing patterns of assessment. After 3 years, there was a need to embrace more adventure in the assessment and the initiative began. I was initially PhD Director then Acting Research Director, which made negotiating change through often mismatched system elements easier. From 2020 and the pandemic, we moved online, and have resumed in hybrid mode.

The initiative required little in the way of *resources* except time, imagination and hard work, but given the pressure on us all to expand higher income generating courses it will always come under pressure for the timetable and room space it occupies given current market pressures. However the lack of an adequate core text was an issue that had to be overcome by providing additional materials and lots of readings. Partly the problem was a compound of the fact that philosophy is little interested in methodology; most methodology texts are technical and little interested in philosophy; and sociological philosophy and methods texts are little interested in management. Contributions made in MOS methods texts are often basic, and frequently are plagued with errors of interpretation when they move further. Positivistic approaches, despite professed neutrality, can be conflictual, focussed on contest, rebuttal, rejection, dismissal, and masculinist – which doesn't make them a welcoming read. Obsession with theory *building* is at the expense of concept generation and what Weick calls *theorising*. Nevertheless our library was highly supportive – especially when I had to read several candidate texts every year for the assessment and select one that was available in ebook format (this was not common in the early stages but is much easier now).

4. The challenges (how and when they were encountered, how they were overcome

One consistent challenge was constant growth, and accordingly change in systems. From 8 staff doing service teaching, with 2 PhD students, in 2004, we are now the largest unit in the University with 250 staff and 3500 students. This brought 4 location changes and high turnover of personnel including key staff with implicit knowledge. It was hard to maintain a culture in which philosophy was central and not an outlier. This has been countered as our current Director of PGR has just returned to the school after a 3 year secondment to the Doctoral Training Partnership and he brings the full weight of his experience and knowledge to support the continuation of the course. There was some normalised opposition - students are performatively oriented, having been trained at school implicitly in positivism, functionalism and realism which seems perfectly natural to them. Some staff too told their students that studying philosophy was irrelevant to their area of study or that they themselves "never had to know this stuff". There was a rejection of critique by some who simultaneously claimed to champion critical thinking, and the inevitable obsession with publication products rather than the thinking skills that lead to good publications. During the pandemic the course on campus skipped a year and we retained and included online resources - ebooks, video materials, philosopher interviews and films. At this time too, there was a change in student complement towards part-time and distance and it became hybrid. We are now moving to a workshop structure again.

5. How the initiative was received by the participants

The participants predictably found the course challenging, to varying degrees, but appreciated that I recognized this through my actual and virtual open-door policy for consultations. Students claimed they never thought that philosophy was so relevant to research, and in some cases they found it (academically and personally) life-changing. Consistently students reported that the model was a reliable road map from which they were able to take bearings as their projects unfolded. Some of them would consult me as they picked up new ideas and wondered whether they were applying them appropriately, or felt they had hit a stumbling block the model could help unlock. This was always done with consent of their supervisors, who I was there to support, in line with our own supervisor development policies, which align with UKCGE recommendations. All students reported enjoying the reading and most reported acquiring new skills in analysis and argumentation. Several former doctoral students are now academics using it including one Business School Dean, one Head of Department in the Netherlands and one in France, and two academics teaching methods in Thailand. Apart from business and management it has been taken up by colleagues in Education and Learning and Occupational Health and used in examining non-conventional cross- disciplinary theses in the Netherlands, Australia and Canada. What they most appreciated though was the practicality of being able to use the assessment vehicle as a case-study experiment to try out and explore - with a degree of safety - how philosophy could be a useful tool to make sense of live research data. What they further reported was how the human interest of the books carried them forward, and got them engaging enthusiastically with ideas they had initially found remote, connecting them with their own practice - this year a student found a hotel in Buenos Aires speaking directly to health service administration in Scotland.

6. The learning outcomes

A professorial external examiner said they would love to do the course content but would be intimidated by the quality of the student assignments. Atomistic forms of feedback miss the most important holistic elements, but standard feedback scores fall between 4.5 and 5/5. Qualitative feedback supports the achievement of *breadth of awareness or understanding* of the range of possibilities in management research, the *appreciation of intellectual depth* behind all approaches, increased *ability to work with colleagues from other disciplines* empathetically improvement in arguing and writing skills, a greater sense of *competence and self-confidence* underpinning their practice, and a renewed *sense of excitement* about research-in-the-world. The assessment vehicle is meant to open up students' thinking about the research process, to get them to appreciate its motility, and the plurality of thinking necessary to engage real world issues - method requires some invention. The best affirmation of this has been invitations to me from other staff to join biannual thesis advisory review panels of students who have followed the course engaged in precisely such complex real world problems - currently one involved in regional trans-agency initiatives in managing the food chain, another working on transdisciplinary gender equality initiatives in universities across the Balkans.

7. Plans to further develop the initiative

Universities across the UK are in dire financial straits. Staff are being terminated, workloads are skyrocketing, pedagogy jettisoned. Marketing administration is frantic. PhD student numbers have been charged to quadruple, with no consideration of subject areas, or capacity for supervision, with workshops replacing longer courses and zoom the norm. How will this affect the teaching of research philosophy? Can it be sold to attract students? It isn't possible to say at present, but it will be affected, and unlikely for the better. It will come under attack from some quarters, and the typologising approaches are likely to prove less easy to defend than those emphasising process and relevance. There are tough times ahead, but this approach has the elements needed to survive, even though it will be forced to change.

First, it needs continuing integration of the model with *newer developments in the field*. Philosophy doesn't change massively but it *does* change. And it *is* practical. Understanding this in MOS typically lags behind other disciplines. Second, continuing search for *understandability*. There are always different ways to say things, helping some people but not others. Third, a *core text* that draws on the experiences we have had and offers more comprehensive practical examples from student research is needed. Finally, this is an introductory course. This always makes it vulnerable if there are insufficient *vertically integrated* advanced courses available that build on it. However, the model can be used with other groups or at *other levels of scalability*.

Because the model focuses on the research process, it is capable of being used to guide the exploration of thinking within any research paradigm, even those that are traditionally unreflexive. So although the level of analysis of this course, and the mode of assessment, are geared to doctoral students, it can be used at any level, although the depth to which the elements of the model can be explored will need to be adapted and adjusted appropriately. Even within the assessment itself there is room for students to focus basically or expansively on the materials and still be successful. I have used it at undergraduate level both with dissertation students, and specialist undergraduate option students studying critical management studies and alternative methods. I have also used it with executive doctoral and MBA students, with a very practical entry point, working in health care settings, law enforcement, financial services, engineering project management, and with consultants involved in action research projects across a variety of industries.

My approach in what can be a highly abstract discipline is to emphasise that philosophers are passionate people - that "philo" means love, which means life and relations beyond isms and typologies. Hempel reminded us that our questions are open; Eco pointed out that our fields are open too. I therefore conclude the course with a story that illustrates how philosophy can be practical, and can even be a matter of life and death. In February 1941, Bergson, whose mother was a Catholic of Irish descent and whose father was a French Jew was still living in Paris although his parents had relocated to England's South Coast. Bergson was non-aligned but drawn to his mother's Catholicism. Because he was a Nobel-prize winner who had helped develop the League of Nations, the Nazi occupiers offered him the opportunity not to register as a Jew. He declined, because he said that it was important those with significant voices aligned with "those about to be persecuted". He didn't single out Jews so it wasn't a matter of beliefs (meontology), bourgeois morality or even identity politics as his increasing identification had been with his mother's Catholicism (to which he converted on his deathbed). It was a matter of values (axiology) and praxis (praxeology). At the age of 81, he queued for hours in the winter cold, caught pneumonia, and died shortly after.

Philosophy is about the decisions we make and the processes by which we make them. This story ends the taught part of the course, but the image of Bergson reminds them as they undertake the assessment journey. As they try to make sense of a weave of multiplicitous data on complex social, organizational and institutional problem situations involving real human actors, it reminds them that seeing other perspectives is not only important, but it may be a matter of life and death - and the future of our world may depend not just on the analytic content of our decisions but on the affective and intuitive processes by which we make them, confronting open questions in an open field.

References

Blaikie, N. (1993/2007) Approaches to Social Enquiry: Advancing Knowledge, Polity Press: Cambridge

Burrell, G, & Morgan, G. (1979) Sociological Paradigms and Organizational Analysis, London: Heinemann

Eric Tsang, E.W.K. (2017) The Philosophy of Management Research London: Routledge

Goodall H.L. Jr (1989) Casing a Promised Land: the Organizational Consultant as Detective

Goodall H.L. Jr (1991) Living in the Rock'n'Roll Mystery: Context, Self and Other as Clues. Carbondale, IL: Southern Illinois University Press

Halfpenny, P. (1982) Positivism and Sociology: Explaining Social Life London: Routledge

Linstead, S. A. (2004) Organization and Postmodern Thought London: Sage

Author Biography

Stephen A. Linstead FAcSS is Professor of Management Humanities at the University of York School for Business and Society. His recent work includes *The Magic of Organization* (2020 ed. with H. Letiche and J-L. Moriceau) and *Viral Verses: Art in Exceptional Times* (ed). And multi award-winning documentary film *Black Snow*.

A Service-learning Approach on Students Consultancy Project: Marketing Research for Breast Cancer Prevention.

Ilia Protopapa
King's Business School, King's College London, London, UK
ilia.protopapa@kcl.ac.uk

Abstract: Students employed marketing research techniques to address causes of fatality of breast cancer. This project adopts a problem-based learning (PLB) approach (Savin-Baden and Major, 2013) that involves students addressing a real problem, the breast cancer. Despite the dreadful consequences, the survival rate of breast cancer is over 99% when it is on stage 1 (KnowYourLemons, 2024). Awareness is lifesaving; however, breast education is not accessible due to its sensitive (censored) nature. This study contributes to the improvement of marketing techniques to raise breast health awareness for breast cancer prevention, to regions where education is not as accessible, through research. This assignment uses experiential learning techniques to offer the students the opportunity to work directly with the external expert, globally organisation 'KnowYourLemons' (KYL). Students are taught research methods to collect data from companies and consumers. The aim is to identify companies (corporate partners) to create partnerships with the NGO to raise awareness of breast health worldwide. Students conducted a mixed method investigation (qualitative via interviews and quantitative research via Qualtrics surveys) to investigate consumers reactions on marketing activities towards promoting breast health and test potential partnerships for KYL. Students analysed their data using qualitative coding and the SPSS statistical software. Then, they pitched their ideas to corporate partners and then to the client (KYL) and to the module leader. Students created an Instagram campaign for the University's social media to promote breast health to the wider student community that was shared through accounts reaching over 18k followers. Finally, this project uses principles of collaborative learning, meaning that students worked in groups of 5-6 students. Collaborative learning helped students to develop teamwork and communications skills and learn from one another. A relevant output of this work is a podcast that was released in 2023 where the module leader, the CEO and Founder of KYL and two students from the best performing groups were interviewed.

1. Introduction

This initiative aims to address the chronic global health issue of breast cancer that remains the leading cancer diagnosis among women worldwide and constitutes a significant cause of mortality in the U.K., through marketing research and education. Despite advancements in medical science that enable a survival rate of over 99% when breast cancer is detected at stage 1 (Know Your Lemons, 2024), the battle is far from won. A lack of widespread awareness and education on breast health, particularly in underrepresented regions make this cancer among the most fatal cancers worldwide. Our initiative recognises that the solution lies not only in medical intervention but also in effective communication and education. Leveraging marketing research, as a critical tool, our objective is to explore and understand the complexities surrounding breast health awareness. We also aim to curate and implement innovative marketing strategies through alliances to eliminate cultural and socioeconomic barriers to raise awareness to places where it is most needed.

To achieve this, we combine academic knowledge through the 'Research in Marketing' core module, part of the MSc in International Marketing at King's College London. Through a partnership with the globally renowned non-profit organization 'KnowYourLemons', students applied their academic learning to a real-world issue under the guidance of Dr Ilia Protopapa, module leader of the 'Research in Marketing' module and Dr. Corrine Beaumont, CEO and Founder of Know Your Lemons. Know Your Lemons makes information beautiful and accessible by using lemons to illustrate how breast cancer may feel, to educate people (see figure 1). Due its accessibility, this campaign became viral to a wide and diverse audience, overcoming the barriers of taboo, fear and literacy that have held breast cancer 'awareness' back for decades (Know Your Lemons website: https://knowyourlemons.org/). KYL's work and impact has been featured in many reputable media such as CNN, BBC, Mashable, and AmericanMarketingAssociation.

Ilia Protopapa

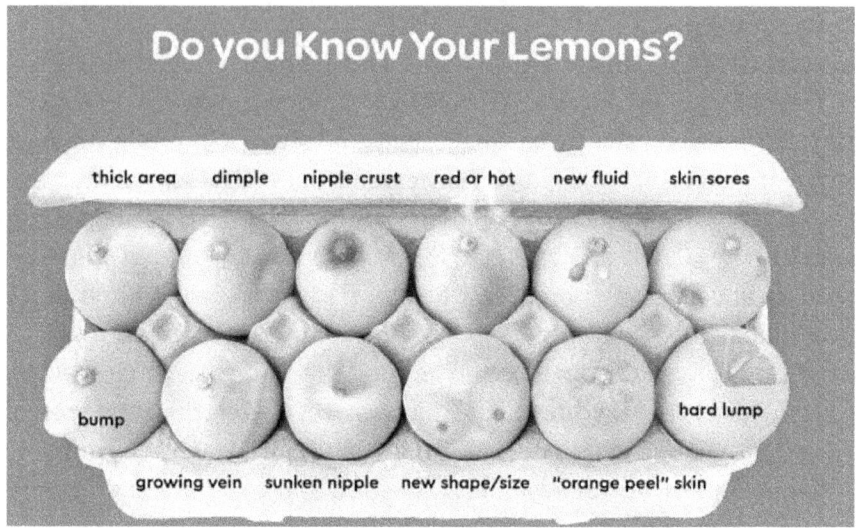

Figure 1 The 'Know Your Lemons' viral campaign.

Backed by bits and pieces of theory, the consultant contributes to practice, whereas the scholar contributes to theory supported by fragments of practice (Gummesson, 2000). Students asked to conduct extensive research and devise marketing strategies that amplify the message of breast health awareness and encourage early detection behaviours through partnering with corporate partners. The focus of the research was the identification of corporate partners that would form alliances with the NGO to promote effective marketing practices for breast health and breast cancer prevention. The initiative aspires to transform the landscape of breast health awareness and ultimately, save lives. This ambitious goal demands not only innovative research methods that students employed to explore appropriate marketing strategies and partners by recruiting potential consumers, but also a commitment to translating our findings into actionable, scalable strategies with a lasting impact for both the NGO and the corporate partner.

This service-learning approach in research methods education is more than an academic endeavour; it aims to equip individuals with the knowledge and tools to take proactive steps towards breast cancer prevention and assist our students into applying research practices into real world problems. The service-learning has been recognised in higher education literature for its effectiveness in enhancing students' academic learning, civic engagement, and personal growth (Eyler & Giles, 1999). Research also shows that service-learning modules such as the Research in Marketing can positively impact students' critical thinking skills as well as the ability to apply theoretical knowledge in practical settings (Bringle & Hatcher, 2009). In this module, the service-learning approach was implemented through a structured program that integrated academic research with practical, community-based projects by partnering with KYL. This method aimed to provide students with hands-on experience in applying their theoretical knowledge to real-world issues, specifically focusing on breast cancer prevention.

2. Research Methods: From theory to practice

The students, as researchers, adopted a mixed method approach that employed exploratory and explanatory research designs to develop a holistic understanding of individuals' awareness and engagement with breast health. Below is an overview of how students have utilised the 'Research in marketing' module in undertaking this consulting project:

Exploratory Qualitative Research: The exploratory research design is used to generate insights that will help define the problem under investigation and to deepen the understanding of consumers' motivations, attitudes and behaviours that are not easy to access using other research methods (Harding, 2013; Hair et al., 2021). For the qualitative part of the research, student researchers reflected and justified the following question: How is qualitative research appropriate to investigate individuals' knowledge towards breast health and cancer? How have individuals been involved with non-profit organisation supporting breast health? Then, the students designed a detailed interview guide to explore individuals' motivations for engaging with breast cancer prevention activities, such as doctor visits and interactions with mobile applications intended to assist breast health. Students conducted a series of semi-structured interviews to capture individuals' inner thoughts, experiences, impressions, and feelings of breast health as well as their perceptions on various partnerships presented between the NGO and the corporate partners. At the end of the qualitative investigation students concluded on the most appropriate corporate partner and marketing idea and prepared a pitch to reach out to the partner to discuss a potential collaboration that can benefit both the NGO and also the Corporate Social Responsibility of the industry partner.

Explanatory Quantitative Research: The explanatory research design frequently uses data collection methods that involve asking respondents structured questions about what they think, feel, and do. Thus, it in the use of survey research methods to collect quantitative data from large groups of people through the question/answer process (Hair et al., 2021). For the quantitative part of the research, researchers reflected and justified the following question: How does quantitative research support the investigation of the challenge? What are the most appropriate promotion techniques to promote breast health awareness? The researchers identified items and scales and design surveys using Qualtrics. The quantitative (explanatory) self-completion online surveys provided student researchers with insights on individuals' awareness of breast health, familiarity with breast cancer prevention activities as well as attitudes towards campaigns promoting breast health and customers' engagement with non-profit organisations. At the end of this investigation students obtain quantitative evidence of the potential success of the partnership and the marketing idea. These data also used in the speech that the students delivered to corporate partners on behalf of the NGO.

How we work with companies to improve health:

Webinars
We offer an interactive online session for employees (and their families) to learn how they can be proactive with their breast health and gain insight to our work and mission and how they can take part.

Volunteer Opportunities
Employees can enroll in our online course to educate in their communities. We also have special projects where employees can donate time and special skills to help us expand our work to new audiences.

Custom campaigns
We work with you to create a custom campaign internally to engage employees throughout the year or during a specific month. This involves educational materials, email templates, employee challenges, etc.

airbnb
"Truly informative and inspiring! We appreciate you taking time to educate us more on breast cancer early detection, and allowing us to realise how so much more needs to be done to spread awareness and get more people informed about this important issue."
—Wei Lin Sen, Airbnb

Nike
"The work you do everyday to spread awareness across the world on Breast Cancer is huge and we're beyond happy that we got the opportunity to partner up with you."
—Livia Silvagni, Nike

crumbl
COOKIES
"This was an incredibly meaningful partnership for our employees and company as a whole. We are elated with the amount of donations from our company and its customers in addition to the number of people educated by the Know Your Lemons Foundation."
—Sawyer Hemsley, Crumbl Cookies

Figure 2 An example from a group's pitch. Ideas presented emerged from students' primary research.

3. The Infrastructure

The foundation of this project is built on a well-coordinated infrastructure that combines pedagogy, research methodology, and technology.

People: The people involved in this project are: the students, the module leader, the CEO and Founder of the NGO, the participants who took part in the primary data collection and lastly the corporate partner. Central to our initiative are the students from King's College London, who bring innovative perspectives and their academic practices to the project. Under the guidance of Dr. Ilia Protopapa and Dr. Corrine Beaumont from 'KnowYourLemons', these students have transitioned from learners to creators, contributing to a cause that extends beyond the classroom. This collaboration is supported by Jacoby's (2015) findings, which highlight the importance of partnerships between educational institutions and community organizations in service-learning programs. Students worked in groups of 5-6 members and had to recruit participants (potential consumers) to test innovative marketing campaigns as a result of a fictitious partnership between the NGO and an identified corporate partner. Following a successful primary data collection, students approach the identified corporate partner to pitch their idea. Their engagement in this project represents a convergence of education and service, with each student group embarking on a journey to not just understand but also apply marketing research practices and theories in a manner that serves the greater good.

Systems: Our project is grounded in a service-learning pedagogy that not only imparts knowledge but also emphasises its application in real-world scenarios. This educational approach, which combines learning objectives with community service, provides a comprehensive learning experience that enhances the students' academic knowledge while instilling a strong sense of civic responsibility. The module incorporated service-learning as a core component of the curriculum, aligning with Eyler and Giles' (1999) model of service-learning, which emphasises the importance of connecting academic content with community service. This approach was designed to enhance students' understanding of research methods through practical application.

Methods: Research is the foundation of our initiative, with a mixed-method approach providing a comprehensive understanding of the complex issue at hand. Through qualitative research via interviews, we delve into the motivations behind individual behaviour regarding breast health, while our quantitative methods via surveys in Qualtrics offer a broader statistical overview of awareness and attitudes. These two methods allowed students to experiment and test different partnerships between the NGO and various corporate partners. This dual-strategy approach ensures a well-rounded analysis, catering to both depth and breadth in our findings. Lastly, students reached out to their selected corporate partners, to pitch their ideas on behalf of the NGO.

Technology: To support our research, we leverage advanced analytical software like SPSS, which allows for sophisticated data analysis and interpretation. Also, students designed their survey in Qualtrics, a professional platform for designing quantitative surveys. Social media platforms serve as our megaphone, broadcasting our message far and wide, to assist the recruitment of participants. Lastly, as part of this initiative students created an Instagram campaign (see figure 3) to raise awareness, this campaign was shared to 18k audience and received positive feedback and engagement. Together, these elements form a robust infrastructure that supports our students in their dual roles as researchers and consultants, enabling them to produce work that is academically sound and socially relevant.

Figure 3 Students' instagram campaign (created and filmed by students) - reached 18k audience.

4. The Challenges

Among various challenges faces, the delicate nature of breast health as a topic of discussion was a main issue that we had to consider. Given the personal and often private connotations associated with this subject, initiating conversations, and encouraging participation required sensitivity and respect for individual comfort levels in qualitative research. To navigate these sensitivities, we implemented recruitment strategies that were both innovative and considerate. QR codes used to promote the purpose of the project and act not only as a technological convenience but also as a mean for potential participants to engage with the project on their own terms. This method provided a discreet and autonomous entry point for individuals to learn about our research and decide independently if they wished to contribute, thereby respecting their privacy.

Moreover, we crafted motivational briefs in qualitative research that were empathetic in tone, designed to resonate with the personal experiences of our audience. These briefs communicated the significance of our work and the tangible impact that participants could have by sharing their insights. By articulating the value of individual contributions to the broader goal of saving lives, we cultivated a sense of communal purpose and agency among participants. Leveraging the broad reach of social media was another strategic move, enabling us to overcome geographical and social constraints. Platforms such as Instagram were used to disseminate information, foster discussions, and build a community united by a common cause. Social media's interactive nature also allowed us to receive feedback, adapt our approach, and sustain engagement over the course of the project. Through these measures, we surmounted the challenges before us, turning each obstacle into an opportunity to refine our methods and deepen our understanding of the societal dimensions of breast health awareness.

4.1 User Reception

Students' experience was evaluated through various means. First, students had to fill in a formal module evaluation for which they scored 4.2/5 [45 out of 108 students]. Then, a dedicated survey asking about students' perceptions of how well this project prepare them for the future and the overall satisfaction towards the project was launched. Findings (n= 83) suggest that the project was perceived positively. More specifically, 81% suggest that this project prepare the well for their future careers while 62% suggest that they were satisfied/ very satisfied with the project (figures 4 and 5).

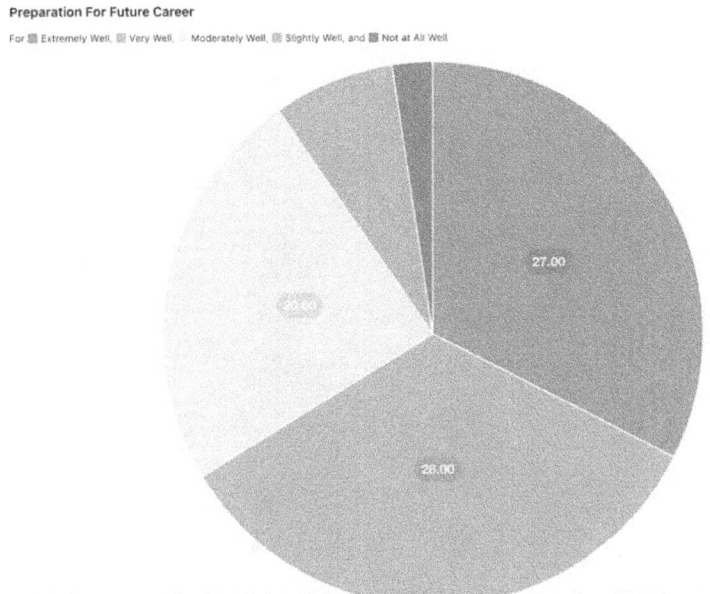

Figure 4 Preparation for Future Career: Survey Outcomes

In addition to the above, this project has been mentioned to the national postgraduate survey (PTES) results in the UK, where students highlight the meaningful project of Know Your Lemons through their qualitative feedback suggesting that this project is *'innovative'*, *'meaningful'* and *'life changing'*.

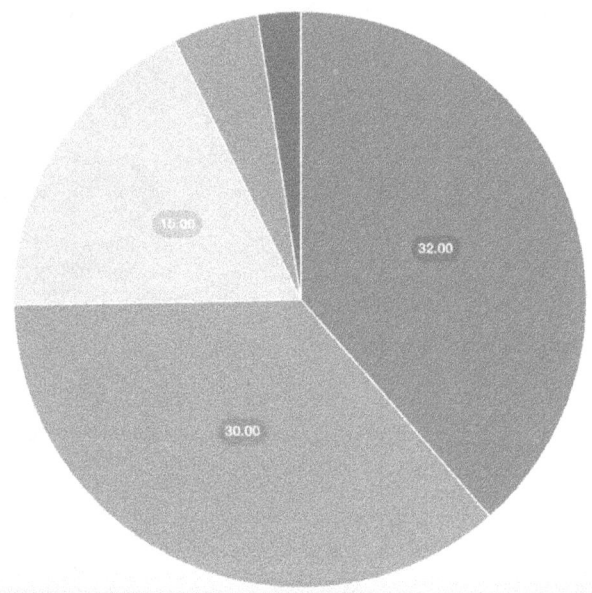

Figure 5 Overall Experience: Survey Outcomes

The Instagram campaign students created and the podcast series that myself, the CEO of the NGO and two students were part of, (see figure 6), saw significant engagement. These initiatives inspired new conversations, encouraged personal stories sharing, and built a community around the shared goal of breast health awareness.

Figure 6 Podcast series on the Research in Marketing consulting project with KYL

The initiative was recognised by peers and leaders in academia garnering awards and nomination such as the Dean's Education Award for "Catalyst for Change for Excellence in EDI" that reflect its innovative approach and meaningful contributions to the field. This positive reception has been a driving force, encouraging us to continue our endeavours and explore new avenues for research and outreach. It is a clear indication that when academic research is aligned with tangible societal needs, the resulting work can resonate deeply within the community and beyond.

5. Learning Outcomes

The learning outcomes of our initiative went beyond the academic realm, illustrating a clear some practical achievements and real-world impact. Below are some key outcomes:

A Significant Partnership Between Students an NGO and Corporate Entities: The collaboration between our students and the NGO partner to create corporate partnerships by pitching to corporate clients demonstrates a commitment into bridging the gap between academia and industry. This partnership facilitated an exchange of ideas, resources, and platforms, enriching the students' learning experience and providing the corporate entity with fresh insights and innovative approaches to social responsibility.

Professional Portfolios that Demonstrated Students' Employability Skills: A tangible outcome of this initiative was the creation of professional portfolios by the students (see figure 7), which showcased their ability to conduct market research, engage with real-world clients, and develop effective marketing strategies. These portfolios assist students to enter the professional world, equipped with a unique blend of theoretical knowledge and applied skills.

Figure 7 An example from a students' portfolio

Substantial Reach and Impact: This process is in line with Bringle and Hatcher's (2009) framework, which suggests that service-learning projects should involve meaningful research activities that benefit both students and the community. As a result of students' involvement in a project asking them to act as consultants to identify relevant marketing campaigns and corporate partners lead to current discussions and future potential collaborations between the identified corporate partner and the NGO. This will significantly impact breast health awareness globally. The Instagram campaign emerged as well as the series of podcasts act as powerful tools for outreach, leveraging the platform's vast user base to spread awareness.

The outcomes were evaluated using a multi-faceted approach. Engagement statistics provided a quantitative measure of the reach and interaction with our campaigns. The quality of student portfolios offered insight into the depth of their learning and the professional competencies they acquired. Feedback from industry partners served as a qualitative barometer for the initiative's relevance and effectiveness in a commercial context. Lastly, students formal quantitative and qualitative feedback evidence the success of this project (see section: user reception).

In sum, the learning outcomes of this initiative reflect a strategic blend of educational objectives met with societal impact that embraces the 'learn by doing' approach by making a difference in the process.

6. Further Development
The plan is to further develop such initiatives with social impact utilising research methods and other fields of expertise. The goal is to create more cross-disciplinary projects that draws on the diverse expertise of our faculty and students. By doing so, we can leverage a wider range of knowledge and perspectives, from marketing strategy to behavioural science, all focused on the critical issue of health awareness or identify other issues that need research and marketing to create awareness of social impact.

Deepening Academic Integration: We aim to potentially integrate this initiative into more modules across our program, beyond the research method. For instance, students specialising in digital marketing could develop online campaigns, while those studying health policy could focus on advocacy and public partnerships. This approach will not only enrich the students' learning experience but also enhance the initiative's capacity to make a meaningful difference.

Widening Corporate Partnerships: We will actively seek out new corporate and NGO partners and deepen existing relationships. These partners are invaluable for providing practical opportunities to our students. By working together, we can reach a wider audience and have a greater impact on public awareness about breast health.

Enhancing Social Media Engagement and Metrics: We also plan to broaden our social media strategy. Social media is a powerful tool for education and engagement, and by leveraging these platforms more effectively, we can encourage more people to learn about breast health, check themselves regularly, and seek medical advice promptly. By expanding our reach and drawing on a broader set of skills and knowledge, we can make a lasting contribution to improving breast health awareness. This isn't just an academic exercise; it is about creating real-world changes.

References

Bringle, R. G., & Hatcher, J. A. (2009). Innovative practices in service-learning and curricular engagement. *New directions for higher education,* 147(147), 37-46.

Eyler, J., & Giles Jr, D. E. (1999). *Where's the Learning in Service-Learning?* Jossey-Bass Higher and Adult Education Series. Jossey-Bass, Inc., 350 Sansome St., San Francisco, CA 94104.

Gummesson, E. (2000). Qualitative methods in management research. Sage.

Hair, J., Ortinau, D., Harrisson, D. E. (2021). *Essentials of Marketing Research.* McGrawHill.

Harding, J. (2013). *Qualitative Data Analysis from Start to Finish.* Sage Publications, Thousand Oaks.

Jacoby, B. (2014). Service-learning essentials: Questions, answers, and lessons learned. John Wiley & Sons.

Know Your Lemons (2024) Breast health isn't talked about. We want to change that. Retrieved February 12, 2024, from https://breastschool.org/about

Savin-Baden, M. (2013). Spaces in between us: a qualitative study into the impact of spatial practice when learning in Second Life. *London Review of Education.*

Author Biography:

 **Dr Ilia Protopapa** is an Assistant Professor of Marketing Education at King's Business School, King's College London. Her areas of interest include diversity and inclusion and GenAI applications in higher education and consumer behaviour. Her recent work was published in the area of consumer behaviour in 'The Handbook of Research on Customer Loyalty' (Edward Elgar Publishing) and higher education for the 'Strategic Brand Management in Higher Education' (Routledge).

Teaching Research Methodologies Through Participatory Performance text

Jocene Vallack
James Cook University, Townsville. Australia
jocene@bigpond.com

Abstract: I have been fortunate to teach qualitative research methodologies at three universities. Drawing on my background in Drama, I began writing the subject content into plays, which I would read aloud with my students. I enjoyed writing up the lessons in this creative format as the students always had a good laugh followed by thoughtful discussion. It was an engaging means to fulfilling the teaching objectives of understanding and evaluating the theoretical structures of the methodologies to be studied. Additionally, the rigor of the methodology under scrutiny could be debated firstly by the characters in the play, and then by the students in discussion. I developed a set of fictional characters to implement the task. Collectively, they were members of an amateur theatre troupe (called the Tragic Floor Theatre Co.) trying to understand and create theatre-in-education about a particular methodology. The characters' egos and errors brought humour to the script, while one character in particular, a retired academic named Professor Citemore, was able to contribute citations from his savant-like, photographic memory. After successful responses to the first play-scripted lessons, the challenge was how to develop more plays and characters to present more methodologies. I realised that the same scenario and cast should be used, as they could be developing a series of theatre-in-education performances about research methodologies. This structure allowed for consistency in character subtext and purpose. Incidental observations of student engagement and laughter during the readings, along with sustained discussion about the embodied methodologies, suggested this was a winning pedagogy worthy of development. This case study will convey how the teaching innovation engages students with research methodologies. It will provide examples of this teaching strategy. It will also offer a template for writing plays about research, which can be adapted by other educators.

1. Introduction

Academic writing can disengage the best of us at times. It is full of terminology that is understood and used in varying ways (sometimes by the same author), while the point of the writing can be buried in unpunctuated paragraphs of obscure grammar. Good researchers who write poorly may be forgiven when the nugget of wisdom is worth searching for. As teachers of research methodologies, we need to clarify the confusion and prepare our students for analysis and evaluation of each approach. Socrates presented his audience with problems to solve and issues to consider through public forum (Beer, 2024). His democratic approach teaches the student to consider the arguments and make an informed evaluation. The play readings aim to teach in this way too.

I write plays about research methodologies. Each of the fictional characters in the play has a motive for being present at a collaborative dialogue about the methodology in question. Each one sees the approach from hir (his or her) own, postmodern perspective, and these perspectives intertwine throughout the play to leave impressions on the student (or reader or audience). The students then can discuss what they have read (or seen on stage), and begin their own collaborative journey in search of the truths. The approach serves to honour the complexity of philosophy and academic debate. Beer quotes Socrates, who maintains:

> *"I am one of those people who would be delighted to be refuted, if I say anything untrue, and who would be delighted to do the refuting if someone else were to say something untrue…. I believe there is no evil so great for a human being as false opinion about the things we are discussing right now. (Beer, 2024)*

2. Context and infrastructure

Last century I was fortunate to be mentored by a wonderful scholar who encouraged me to take the sorts of risks in qualitative research that have now become more widely accepted. He had worked with Robert Stake at the University of Illinois when Stake was creating the new and controversial methodology he called 'Case Study'. He worked, too, with Norman Denzin who was at that time exploring Performance Text as methodology. My mentor, the late Dr Darrel Caulley OAM, created the Association for Qualitative Research in 2000. I shadowed his progress, and he encouraged me to publish my student efforts in the peer reviewed journal, which grew to be classed as an ERA rated

A journal. My first published play was a book review, written in response to Denzin's innovative publication titled, Performance Ethnography Critical Pedagogy and the Politics of Culture(Denzin, 2003) In the play the characters were members of an amateur theatre group who were preparing to present the content of this academic book as a theatre performance. The characters included actors (with the egos), the director (with the 'vision'), a PhD student (with some contextual understanding), a retired academic with a photographic memory for quotations and an alcoholic journalist who just wanted the outline for tomorrow's paper. Various views about what is important in Denzin's book are presented via the conversations. The characters argue over meaning and significance of various sections, and the audience is presented with an overview of the content and issues. This work was the foundation for my more recent presentations of methodologies through play writing.

3. Challenges and outcomes

One of the main challenges for playwrights is finding a receptive audience. As this endeavour began as notes for my class, I already had a captive audience. But it did develop a little beyond that. In 2001 and 2005, I was honoured to have two of my plays about research methodology performed by university students as a feature at conferences for the Association of Qualitative Research. The scripts were crafted to be comical yet informative, and the musical genre was well received as a break from the otherwise more laboured content of the proceedings. It became apparent that this was good pedagogy. The characters explained their ideas and argued for their interpretations. It was like a court case in action, and the audience members could make their judgements at the end of it. Moreover, the audience could continue the banter, in Socratic fashion, over morning tea.

When teaching research methodology to graduate students as a volunteer in Tanzania, I wrote another play with my students about Narrative Inquiry. It showcased the powerful stories of local folk (Vallack *et al.*, 2010). This play dealt with sombre themes of war and danger, which mandated a more appropriately sensitive genre. The panache of the play needs to align with its purpose.

This case study has evolved as a longitudinal study of play writing as a means to presenting engaging content to students of qualitative methodology. For classroom and seminar use, short plays written in comic genre are ideal. The play about Action Research (McTaggart, 1994) is a good example. There was always a lot of laughter, and funny voices were encouraged. Here is an excerpt from the play about Acton Research Methodology:

3.1 Stage directions:
This play is set and staged in a public bar. The audience sit at tables, and the players move about the room, but locate themselves primarily in the bar area, on high stools. Citemore is serving at the bar. Jane is cleaning tables from time to time. Blah Blah sits dishevelled and partially inebriated at a stool in the corner. He takes notes throughout the proceedings. He is at home here. The Chorus sit in pairs at two back tables. They are hecklers.

3.2 Characters:

Director	Con Sergeivich
Stage Manager	Jane
Actor	Histrionica Chat
Academic	Professor Citemore
Critic	Blah Blah
Student Teacher	Cassandra Rush
Chorus	4 cheerful patrons

(The Philosophers' Drinking Song is playing. Con gestures to Citemore to reduce the volume.)

3.3   Scene 1

Con: Thanks for coming at such short notice. I have good news for you – we are to become educators! The university has asked us to demonstrate Action Research – show 'em what it's all about! Now Citemore used to be an academic, before he retired, so he will guide us. Cassandra, too, can help. She's at Teachers' College, and it's all the rage there.

Histrionica: I'm an actor! What's it got to do with me me me?

Con: Actors are researchers.

Citemore: (jovially) Can you substantiate that claim?

Con: Our humble little theatre company, "Tragic Floor"...

Jane: Can we change the name –

Con: ...is to be funded by the Department of Education to enlighten and empower communities with the tool of Action Research.

Chorus: What a tool!

Con: Indeed. We will now need to teach ourselves how to teach the teachers to teach Action Research! Any questions?

Blah Blah: There had better be a good story in this – or I'm wasting good drinking time.

Con: Just the usual – quest, passion, downfall, resilience – the mother's story, the father's story, the hero's story –

Blah Blah: Get on with it.

Cassandra: I thought this was about teachers as researchers - improving pedagogy.

Con: That's the treasure we all seek, but of course there is first the journey-

Histrionica: Thwart with trickery, bigotry and dogma – laced with humour, romance...

Citemore: Dignity and *Ethical Clearance* forms. Oh, excuse me. Here. Action Research:

> "...the cyclic dynamic of planning, acting, observing and reflecting..."(McTaggart, 1991),

> or this:

"Action Research is the systematic study of attempts to improve educational practice by groups of participants by means of their own practical actions and by means of their own reflection upon the effects of those actions." Ebbutt,1985.(Arung, 2015)

Histrionica: There's no mystery to Action Research. It's just PLAN, ACT,

REFLECT, PLAN, ACT, REFLECT, PLAN...

Chorus member PLAN, ACT, REFLECT, PLAN...woops! I overacted!

Citemore: Yes, all right. Any parrot can quote that, but WHAT DOES IT MEAN?

The opening of the play sets out the fictional context and introduces both the characters and the topics for discussion. Each character speaks from hir own subjective standpoint, as they attempt to ultimately establish a common understanding of the Action Research methodology. Their efforts serve those of the audience, as both characters and audience all strive to comprehend the methodology.

Later in the play the characters discuss the equality of status among the research participants, and how this allows for grass roots data, which may provide new insights that are potentially unseen through a top-down approach:

Histrionica: Wait! Planning? How do we plan?

Jane: Now this is my territory. I'm ok with the logistics. You have a small group of committed participants who meet on a regular basis. Is that it?

Con: Well done! And each member of the group, each *participant,* has equal status in that group. Each person's view is heard and considered by the group, regardless of his or her workplace status.

Histrionica: So, Con doesn't have any more power that me, even though he's the Director?

Citemore: That's correct.

Cassandra: And you discuss possibilities collaboratively – there is healthy debate, and everyone supports the group's decision in the end.

Jane: What if they are wrong!

Con: Right and wrong are values not facts. We test the values through our group discussion.

Jane: I really don't get this.

Histrionica: You're just scared because it's taking you out of your comfort zone.

Jane: What if our plan doesn't work? We've failed!

Citemore: Herein lies the beauty of it all. If our evidence suggests that our plan has not led us to a desirable change, we try again. Simple really.

Blah Blah: How many restarts can you have?

Citemore: As many as you can fit into the time.

Blah Blah: Or the budget?

Citemore: There is that.

Con: Possibly, but these things are all considered by the group.

Histrionica: When do we act?

Cassandra: As soon as we can. Neville Johnson says: " <u>Not</u> READY- AIM- FIRE , <u>but rather</u> READY- FIRE- AIM!"

Jane: What's that mean?

Blah Blah: Who's Neville Johnson?

Citemore: He's an old colleague of mine from Melbourne University.

Histrionica: READY – FIRE - AIM – That's what I do all the time. I act impulsively!

Cassandra: Well we don't have to be quite as dynamic as you.

Histrionica: No, because I've been trained at...

Cassandra: So you said.

The group does plan, but they shouldn't take too long to act. Neville Johnson warns against this. He says if we take too long, it's "READY- AIM- CHRISTMAS HOLIDAYS! "

Con: Our first actions do not have to be perfect. We try something and then assess it and retry it with modifications – like we have always done when during our play rehearsals.

Histrionica: Exactly. Like rehearsing a play. During the rehearsal time, which is really a type of Action Research, we PLAN- ACT- OBSERVE- REFLECT. When I get the script, I assess it and interpret it. Then I take my interpretation to the rehearsal and try it out with the group of other actors.

Con: And they, too, have brought their interpretations and impressions to the rehearsal.

Histrionica: Then I act – we all do – together. Con and Jane have observed my acting. And we observe each other as well. Con's made notes –

Citemore: He has evidence to support his suggestions – "that didn't work because..." – that sort of thing.

Histrionica: I don't think he'd need to say that.

4. Learning outcomes for the author

The more I use theatre to introduce methodology to graduate students and peers, the more I see the pedagogical value in this arts-based approach. The characters voice the doubts and confusion that may be experienced by the learners as they muddle their ways through to understanding each theoretical framework. Like all of us, they come with the baggage of their perspective. Histrionica is egotistical and insecure, but brave and seeks authenticity in what she does; Jane is precise and cautious and afraid of getting it wrong; Citemore is knowledgeable but does not show flair for synthesis and creativity like some others. Individually, like us all, they have weaknesses but together, their combined skills can see a way through the maze of the approach. It was important to develop a cast with varying abilities to showcase different perspectives. I believe I have now created a working formula with which to move forward and teach other methodologies.

5. Learning outcomes for the students

I have used the play about Action Research methodology several times in postgraduate classes and in arts-based, research seminars, such as the recent CARTA (Creative Arts Research Training Academy) symposium in Cairns, Australia. Apart from offering a welcome break from conventional delivery methods, which usually requires a lot of passive listening on the students' part, the plays present both agreed and controversial characteristics about research methodologies. These can generate group discussion and, where appropriate, Socratic rebuttal. I encourage students and colleagues to use the plays as templates for writing their own theatrical presentations of the methodologies in need of examination. It is a way of engaging higher order thinking skills in one's learning. And it's fun.

6. Developing the case study

In the next twelve months I hope to review and update my knowledge on popular approaches to qualitative research in preparation for further play writing. Many new approaches, including my own creation, Soliloquy Methodology (Vallack, 2021), have emerged since I started teaching in the area. I will then attempt to incorporate the selected information into a new book of plays. The book may be used as supplementary reading for a course in qualitative research methods, or just as one-off readings in academic seminars. It would be especially positive to see some of the plays performed at academic conferences, as they were in the past. Dramatic Arts students are particularly good at this.

7. Conclusion

As a teacher of five decades duration, I have observed that students engage with information that is relevant to their needs and learning methods that make them feel included. Reading plays together for a laugh, for a discussion and for debate is a useful means for synthesising given content in a scholarly manner. I strongly contend that methodology should be aligned and consistent in its structure, and that the researchers who use it should understand the anatomy of the approach they are choosing. Is it the best fit for their research questions? Reading a set of plays together with one's classmates is quick and potentially enjoyable. It is also a way for new researchers to see a big picture view of available methods. The researcher can then choose a methodology and in earnest, begin to study and evaluate its potential.

References

Arung, F. (2015) 'The conceptual framework of classroom Action Research'. *English education program of teachers' training and education faculty.* https://usnpendbing.wordpress.com/tag/action-research

Beer, A. (2024) 'Socrates on the blessing of being refuted'. *Antigone,* https://antigonejournal.com/2022/2001/socrates-being-refuted/.

Denzin, N. (2003) Performance ethnography: Critical pedagogy and the politics of culture. U.S.A.: Sage.

McTaggart, R. (1994) 'Participatory Action Research: issues in theory and practice'. , *Educational Action Research,* 2 (3), pp. 313-317.

Vallack, J. (2021) Changing art into research: Soliloquy Methodology. 1st edn. London: Routledge.

Vallack, J. *et al.* (2010) 'News from Dodoma: A play about research in Tanzania'. *Association for Qualitative Research,* 2010 Cairns, Australia.

Author Biography

Dr Jocene Vallack; During an academic career spanning over two decades, Jocene has worked as a Research Fellow, an Academic Advisor, and lectured in Research Methodology, directing and acting. Her publications total approximately thirty, solo-authored papers, chapters and a book - Vallack, J. (2021*) Changing Arts into Research: Soliloquy Methodology* (Routledge: London).

Students as Researchers: Fostering Research and Analytical Skills Through Interdisciplinary Approaches

Sandra Vasconcelos [1] Carla Melo[2] António Melo[3] Dália Liberato[4] and Maria Carlos Lopes[5]

[1]School of Hospitality and Tourism, Polytechnic of Porto, Vila do Conde Portugal; CIDTFF - Research Centre on Didactics and Technology in the Education of Trainers; UNIAG – Applied Management Research Unit

[2]ESHT, Polytechnic of Porto, Vila do Conde Portugal, UNIAG, Applied Management Research Unit, CiTUR, Centre of Tourism Research, Development and Innovation

[3]ESHT, Polytechnic of Porto, Vila do Conde, Portugal, CiTUR, Centre of Tourism Research, Development and Innovation, CIDTFF, Research Centre on Didactics and Technology in the Education of Trainers

[4]ESHT, Polytechnic of Porto, Vila do Conde Portugal, UNIAG, Applied Management Research Unit, CiTUR, Centre of Tourism Research, Development and Innovation

[5]Lamego Higher School of Technology and Management, Polytechnic of Viseu, CiTUR (Centre for Research, Development and Innovation in Tourism

s.vasconcelos@esht.ipp.pt; carlamelo@esht.ipp.pt; antonio.melo@esht.ipp.pt; dalialib@esht.ipp.pt; mcslopes@estgl.ipv.pt

ORCIDs: 0000-0003-4062-331X; 0000-0003-3097-4108; 0000-0001-7572-0545; 0000-0003-0513-6444; 0000-0002-1903-5532

Abstract: Focussing on an assignment developed at the School of Hospitality and Tourism (Portugal), this entry describes an interdisciplinary project involving 3rd year Tourist Activities Management students, who were challenged to carry out practical research activities on stakeholders' current perceptions on the most valued soft skills. Based on a segmented approach focusing on different industry subsectors, the project aimed to not only identify key market skills, but also foster pedagogical innovation and flexibility by supporting the adoption of participatory approaches and assert the value of tourism studies and research within the industry. Bearing in mind the different stages of research and content analysis processes, participants first had to identify relevant stakeholders within different tourism subsectors, as to collect and analyse their perceptions. In addition to contacting, preparing, and carrying out multiple interviews, they were required to analyse the data collected and write a short paper outlining their work and presenting their findings, which were then discussed in an open forum (final oral presentations). Stemming from different areas, faculty members acted as facilitators having supported students through networking activities and multiple topical sessions, ranging from issues underpinning qualitative design to webinars with external experts and workshops on data collection techniques and content analysis. Additionally, different monitoring sessions were held to discuss the groups' progress. Having involved 5 different courses, this joint project resulted in a collection of 12 research papers that were developed and assessed collaboratively by students and facilitators. In addition to a positive impact on students' motivation, the project enhanced students' soft skills through research activities, at the same time it bridged the gap between academia and the tourism and hospitality sector.

1. Introduction

The following entry refers to an interdisciplinary project carried out at the School of Hospitality and Tourism involving 3rd year Tourist Activities Management students. Focusing on identifying the soft skills most valued by the different subsectors of the Tourism and Hospitality industries, its main goals were two-fold: to develop students' critical and interpersonal skills by having them reflect on the characteristics and demands of each subsector and the ensuing challenges; and to foster research and analytical skills, involving students in a collaborative research project that encompassed and put into practice some of the approaches, techniques and instruments introduced in research methodology courses.

The idea for the project originated from the team of teachers, who felt a need to engage students involve them in research activities which they would perceive as relevant for their future. On the one hand, having previously attended research methodology courses, students had shared their doubts on research methodology's practical applications, mostly seeing it as a restrictive field, only applicable in very specific academic settings such as, for example, school assignments. On the other hand, they also lacked knowledge on job profiles and skills, making it necessary to work on this topic. This assumption, which was supported by recent reports identifying key skills in today's market (e.g., Future of Jobs Report 2023, Future of Education and Skills 2030) (WEF, 2023; OECD, 2019), and the need to foster students' awareness on their pivotal role, as well as the role universities and other institutions can play within this scope, paved the way for the project.

Even though interdisciplinary projects are becoming increasingly common in Tourism Education, this project can be described as original and innovative in that: 1) it challenges students to carry out applied research based on interactions with industry stakeholders; and 2) its main topic – soft skills – has become increasingly relevant, particularly given the current situation of the tourism and hospitality industry. The COVID- 19 pandemic, paired with recent economic and technological changes, has taken a toll on the tourism and hospitality industries, having significantly impacted its ability to hire and retain professionals that meet the current needs of the market. As consumers (i.e., travellers) become more demanding and new trends emerge, the unprecedented staff and skills shortage experienced by the tourism and hospitality industry have prompted changes in what is expected from professionals and graduates within this scope, with different studies acknowledging the need for enhanced curricula that hinge on a closer collaboration between schools and the market (Guden & Safaeimanesh, 2024; Deale, 2020). This collaboration should impact not only program design, but also reflect on the development of experiential activities and applied research (Čuić Tanković, Kapeš & Kraljić, 2021; Pranić, Pivčević & Praničević, 2021).

In addition to bridging the gap between academia and the industry (by prompting U-I collaboration) and promoting a joint reflection regarding the importance of soft skills, the project, whose main outputs were a research paper based on interviews with stakeholders stemming from different subsectors within the industry and its public discussion, relied on collaboration and interdisciplinarity, having included 5 different courses. In simpler terms, students' work should not only focus on soft skills, but allow them to develop those same skills, by working collaboratively in authentic and multifaceted settings.

This project has, therefore, enabled research to be carried out in the tourism and hospitality sector, demonstrating the link between fundamental and applied research in the sector, guaranteeing a perspective of problematization and usefulness in terms of the career market, contacted with the real needs of companies in terms of soft skills and the usefulness of discussing them, both for students and the sector.

In the following sections the authors will briefly outline the initiative by giving a general overview of the activities carried out and describing the required infrastructure (including the people involved, the different sessions that have taken place and the software used in the different activities), the challenges faced (and how they were overcome), overall reception, key learning outcomes and plans to further develop the initiative.

2. Infrastructure

2.1 Project Overview

The Interdisciplinary Project described in this entry sought to reinforce students' knowledge of soft skills and how they are perceived and valued within the different tourism and hospitality subsectors, while providing them with opportunities for carrying out applied research within the scope of their studies and for developing transferrable skills, namely collaboration, critical thinking, and communication.

Being the first time students developed a project involving so many different courses (previous projects involved up to 3 courses, often consisting of multiple assignments, whereas this was structured in a way students had to submit and present 1 paper for all the participating courses), this was considered an innovative approach, that combined technical, research and soft skills

Working in groups of 3-6 members, students were challenged to write and present short papers (<5000 words) on soft skills, based on previously defined set of guidelines and template (see Table 1).

Table 1. General Project Guidelines (Vasconcelos et al., 2022a)

Soft Skills & Tourism: From the market to academia	Span:	March – April 2021 (Summer Semester)
	Groups:	3 – 6 students* * The minimum required number of interviews will depend on the number of students in the groups
	Output 1	Written Assignment Short paper (<5000 words + abstract in English and Portuguese) Subsectors: Travel Agencies & Tour Operators Entertainment & Events DMO (Destination Management Organization) Accommodation
	Output 2	Oral Presentation (in English)

The focus of each paper (i.e., the subsector each group would work on) was based on the elective courses students were taking (Tourist Destination Management, Management of Travel Agencies and Tour Operators, Quality Management in Tourism or Hotel Management), with other courses (such as English Applied to Tourism) providing support for developing the final outputs.

Aligned with the different stages of research and content analysis processes, the groups must first review recent literature on soft skills within the scope of the tourism and hospitality and their assigned subsector, based on research of published articles in the SCOPUS and WoS databases. In addition to framing their work, this review should also underpin the interview script to be applied to stakeholders from the different fields, based on the literature review. Students must, therefore, identify and contact relevant stakeholders within each subsector, to collect and analyse their perceptions, as well as prepare and carry out multiple interviews, which were then transcribed and analysed resorting to content analysis. The final short paper should outline their work and present key findings, which were also discussed in an open forum (final oral presentation), including the opportunity for the educational community to participate.

In short, besides an abstract (written in English and Portuguese), the short paper should include a background section, consisting of literature review focusing on soft skills and their relevance within the scope of tourism and the selected subsector, a case study (based on the interviews and ensuing analysis) and a conclusion (Figure 1).

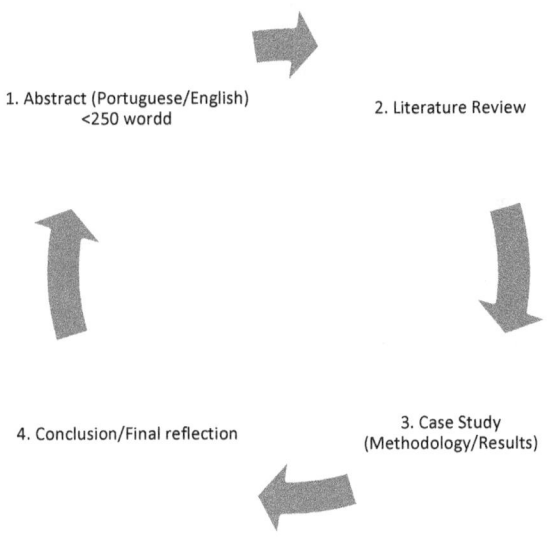

Figure 1. Short Paper – key sections

To support their work, in addition to tutorial sessions (to monitor and provide feedback), students had access to additional materials (e.g., worksheets, guidelines and templates) and were given the opportunity to take part in debates and seminars with experts from different areas. This support was spread over the span of the project making it possible to address ongoing issues and challenges (Figure 2).

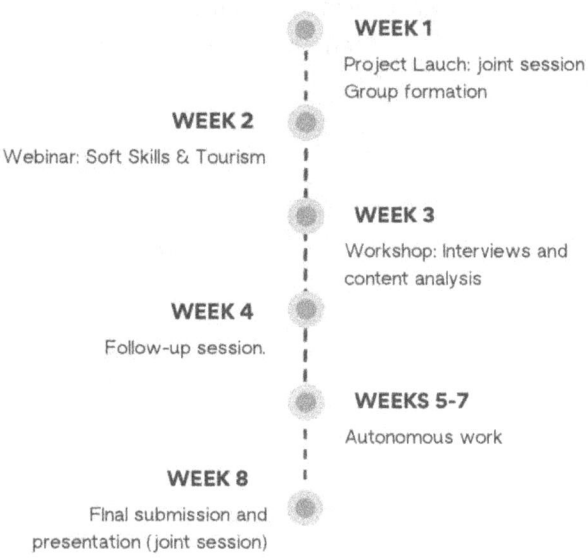

Figure 2. Project Timeline

2.2 People and Support Sessions

The project involved 52 students of the third year Tourist Activities Management, attending 5 different Curricular Units (Tourist Destination Management, Management of Travel Agencies and Tour Operators, Hotel Management, Quality Management in Tourism and English Applied to Tourism VI). Students were initially divided into 13 groups, with 12 having submitted and presented the final research paper. 6 faculty members were involved in the project, having been responsible for designing the activities, as well as monitoring and assessing students' work, during the semester.

As summarized in Table 2, considering the elective courses attended by the students and the different tourism and hospitality subsectors, students interviewed 45 stakeholders, having identified 5 key (transversal) soft skills.

Table 2. Number of groups and interviews by subsector

Subsector	Tourism animation and Events	Destination Management Organizations	Accommodation	Travel Agencies and Tour Operators
No. of groups	2	3	4[3]	4
No. of Interviews	8	8	16	13

The titles and scope of the papers reflected the groups' different perspectives, making it possible to identify specific skills within each subsector (Table 3).

Table 3. Students' short papers grouped by subsector

	Subsector	Title
Short Papers	Destination Management Organizations (3)	The Importance of soft skills in DMOs
		Soft skills in tourism: the case of Porto's Tourism Association, the Municipalities of Bragança and Figueira da Foz and the Regional Tourism Board of the Azores
		Soft skills and their key role in DMOs
	Travel Agencies and Tour Operators (4)	The importance of Soft Skills in travel agencies and tour operators
		Soft skills and tourism – From the market to academia: soft skills in travel agencies
		The rise of soft skills: the tourism sector's perspective
		The added value of soft skills in travel agencies: the importance of qualified human resources
	Tourism Animation and Events (2)	Interpersonal skills in tourism – events management
		Soft skills and team building
	Accommodation/Hotels (3)	Soft skills in hotels
		Soft skills in Portuguese hotels: the hotel managers' perspectives
		Soft Skills and the hospitality industry: a qualitative study on the most valued competences in Portuguese hotels

Drawing from students' papers and ensuing reflections, communication, flexibility, resilience, empathy and teamwork emerged as the skills currently more valued by industry stakeholder, with flexibility standing out as the most transversal skill (in that it crosscuts the different subsectors). As for resilience,

---

[3] Of the 4 initial groups only 3 submitted the final short paper.

students determined that the need for this still became more apparent following the COVID-19 pandemic (Vasconcelos et al., 2022b; Vasconcelos et al., 2022c).

The identification and ensuing categorization of key skills is indicative of students analytical and critical work, in that they were able to not only collect, but also interpret and reflect on the data. Even though most interviewees did not directly cite empathy as a key skill, for example, students were able to establish this category, based on examples provided (mostly pertaining to customer service and friendliness).

2.3 Software

Even though students were given the possibility to choose what software to use to record and transcribe the interviews and analyse data, project workshops provided an overview of standard content analysis software (WebQDA and NVivo) as well as alternative tools, such as Microsoft Excel.

The project's launch, webinar and workshops were held over Zoom.

To support the submission of the short papers, a designated area was created in the institutional Learning Management System (i.e., Moodle) in which the guidelines, examples, templates and relevant links were made available for students.

3. Challenges

Based on observation and on students' perceptions (collected by means of two questionnaires applied at the beginning and at the end of the project), the challenges faced can be grouped into two categories. On the one hand, the challenges faced by facilitators, and, on the other, those highlighted by students.

From the teachers' perspective, collaborative work was sometimes perceived as difficult, as there was a need to integrate different content and perspectives. This was overcome by holding several preparatory meetings and careful design, which involved developing and agreeing on outcomes, guidelines and templates. When it came to teaching research methods, teachers must also play to their strengths, with each team member focussing on specific areas (e.g., preparing and conducting interviews, analysing data and academic writing). It was also necessary to overcome students' initial reaction to the project by motivating and helping them contact stakeholders and gain their confidence. Initially, the focus on research methodologies was regarded with mistrust, not only due to the project itself, but also because none of the teachers were, in fact, associated with previous research methodology courses. This segmented view on research and particularly research instruments and data analysis had to be overcome by offering a holistic and integrative overview of the research process and its potential outcomes and relevance.

For students, based on the data retrieved in the questionnaires, time management was the most significant concern, with 65.7% of respondents, admitting they struggled with it. It should be noted that in addition the project, students had other course-specific assignments and assessment, which may have contributed to this perception and should be addressed in future iterations. Other challenges pertained to scheduling and conducting the interviews (mentioned by 40.0% of respondents) and content analysis (31.4%). This could point to the need of holding additional sessions and improving communication. Notwithstanding, groups were able to complete the assignment having succeeded and passing the different courses.

4. How the initiative was received by the users or participants

When comparing the responses of the initial and final questionnaires, students consider the project to have been successful (100% of respondents considered that it added value to their learning experience and endorsed the approach). Overall, students considered that the project supported the development of a wide range of competences, particularly when it comes to research skills, the use of technical language, teamwork, collaboration, and communication, adapting and managing time efficiently, something that was also highlighted by facilitators.

Another perceived benefit of the project relates to the fact students could focus on only one project (as opposed to different assignments, usually one per each participating course), by identifying and learning the interaction and connection between the subjects of the different curricular units. In addition to favoring in-depth work, rather than relying on a more segmented approach, this allowed students to concentrate and manage their time better. This concentration, paired with the webinar, workshops and monitoring sessions also allowed facilitators to gain a better understanding of the groups' progresses, having resulted in a closer and more productive relationship.

For teachers, having to work collaboratively and articulate content and assessment strategies, helped them acknowledge the complementarity of each of the areas involved, which ultimately resulted in a better mutual understanding. Given the complexity of the project and the need for continuous monitoring, teamwork was also key to assure that every group received timely feedback.

5. Learning outcomes

As detailed in section 2.1., the project yielded 12 short research papers. Using qualitative approaches, students developed case studies having had the opportunity to prepare and carry out interviews and analysing data (resorting to content analysis).

Considering the project's focus on research, both the facilitators and students' perceptions suggest that it succeeded in enhancing participants research skills, namely when it comes to designing effective data collection instruments and the ensuing data analysis.

The project also raised students' awareness to the importance of soft skills in the industry (88.6% of inquired students considered the activities carried out helped become more familiar with the theme) and to the key role played by Higher Education Institutions within this scope (97.1% positive answers). All the students who completed the final questionnaire (100%) recognized the importance of these skills in enhancing employability and career progression, having shown interest in further developing their skillset (Vasconcelos et al., 2022a; 2022b).

Regarding assessment, even though students were expected to submit only one assignment and make a joint presentation, given the different requirements and estimated coursework of the courses involved, each facilitator defined the dimensions and their overall weight in their course's assessment (Table 4).

Table 4. Assessment: Assessed dimensions and relative weight (by course)

Curricular Units	%	Assessed Dimensions and weight
English Applied to Tourism VI	25%	Abstract – 10% Presentation – 15%
Tourism Destination Management	60%	Literature Review/Case Study* – 50% Presentation – 10%
Quality Management in Tourism	40%	Literature Review/Case Study* – 30% Presentation – 10%
Management of Travel Agencies and Tour Operator	40%	Literature Review/Case Study* – 30% Presentation – 10%
Hotel Management	40%	Literature Review/Case Study* – 30% Presentation – 10%

*Elective courses

Even though students could choose to write the short paper in English or Portuguese, the abstract and presentation must be in English (accounting for 25% of the course's final grade). As for other courses, the relative weight of the project on students' assessment was left to the teachers' discretion. Notwithstanding, the projects overall assessment was carried out collaboratively, with teachers being in attendance and taking part in the papers' presentation and discussion.

In addition to these outcomes, the project was also successful in supporting the development of research skills. Drawing from the questionnaires and teachers' observation, as well as the short papers written and presented by students, the activities carried out were instrumental in developing students' information literacy, as they were able to find, evaluate and use information from reliable sources, using established databases and citing other authors/research, as well as their critical thinking, in that they succeed in engaging in reflexive writing and discussing not only their finding, but also the process leading up to the final paper and presentation. This was also indicative of their written and presentation skills.

Having collected and interpreted data using specific software, as well as taken part in dedicated workshops, participants also developed their data analysis skills, having become familiar with various research methods and techniques, and able to draw meaningful conclusions. Working in groups and considering the different stages of the project and its complexity, students had the opportunity to expand their problem-solving abilities, breaking down problems into manageable steps and asking for guidance and support when necessary.

6. Plans to further develop the initiative

The development of an interdisciplinary project by final-year undergraduate tourist activities management students, albeit demanding, succeeded in augmenting students' personal and academic skills, particularly at a time they were about to start their work placements and be in direct contact with the labour market.

In addition to the importance of soft skills, participants highlighted the opportunity to carry out a research project and the fact they had to actually write and discuss an academic paper, with some going insofar as considering this opened their minds to new possibilities, particularly to pursuing a master's degree.

The project also succeeded in promoting learner autonomy, not only by encouraging further reflection on the approaches used and the solutions found by each group, but also by making it possible to identify aspects to be improved (e.g., time management, data collection and analysis) which can be tackled in future initiatives. Furthermore, students were able to find shortcomings in how soft skills are being addressed within the scope of tourism curricula, which suggests further research on the topic.

As a result, regarding future work, it is expected that facilitators repeat the initiative in upcoming semesters, making slight improvements (given the balance at the end of the semester), particularly when it comes to communication with students, as well as increasing the number of mentoring sessions to ensure that participants are able to keep up with the different tasks. In hindsight, it would also have been more useful to hold the interview and content analysis workshop later in the semester or have a second workshop once the students had actually started transcribing and analyzing the interviews.

All in all, however, the project is believed to have a strong replicability and transferability potential, with the guidelines and templates developed being adaptable to other settings, paving the way for similar initiatives in other scopes.

This project has opened up research opportunities in the tourism and hospitality sector, demonstrating the link between fundamental and applied research in the sector, guaranteeing a perspective of problematization and usefulness in terms of entering the labor market, contact with the real needs of companies in respect of soft skills and the usefulness of discussing them, both for the students and for the industry. It should also be added that some of the participants were able to establish a rapport with stakeholders, having extended their networks, with 4 of them having completed their work placements in companies that haven taken part in the project.

References

Čuić Tanković, A., Kapeš, J., & Kraljić, V. (2021). Importance of Soft Skills and Communication Skills in Tourism: Viewpoint from Tourists and Future Tourism Employees. Tourism in Southern and Eastern Europe, 6, 167-185. https://doi.org/10.20867/tosee.06.12

Deale, C. S. (2020). Students as Researchers: Learning about Tourists of the Future. Journal of Hospitality and Tourism Education, 32(1). https://doi.org/10.1080/10963758.2019.1654888

Guden, N., & Safaeimanesh, F. (2024). Conclusion: what should be the role of tourism education social structures to create and support collaborative learning environments and the tourism sector? Worldwide Hospitality and Tourism Themes, 16(1). https://doi.org/10.1108/WHATT-02-2024-0021

OECD. (2019). OECD Future of Education and Skills 2030 - OECD Learning Compass 2030. https://www.oecd.org/education/2030-project/contact/OECD_Learning_Compass_2030_Concept_Note_Series.pdf

Pranić, L., Pivčević, S., & Praničević, D. G. (2021). Top 30 soft skills in tourism and hospitality graduates: A systematic literature review. Tourism in Southern and Eastern Europe, 6, 637-656. https://doi.org/10.20867/tosee.06.43

Vasconcelos, S., Melo, A., Melo, C., Liberato, D., & Lopes, M. C. (2022). Soft Skills in Action: Developing Tourism Students Skills Through Interdisciplinarity. In J. V. de Carvalho, P. Liberato, & A. Peña (Eds.), Advances in Tourism, Technology and Systems (pp. 203–213). Smart Innovation, Systems and Technologies, vol 284. Springer Nature Singapore. https://doi.org/10.1007/978-981-16-9701-2_17

Vasconcelos, S., Melo, C., Melo, A., & Liberato, D. (2022). Interdisciplinarity in Action: Developing Students' Soft Skills Through Project-Based Learning and Field Work. In L. G. Chova, A. L. Martínez & I. C. Torres (Eds.), INTED2022 Proceedings (pp.4852–4859). IATED Academy. https://doi.org/10.21125/inted.2022.1267

Vasconcelos, S., Melo, C., Melo, A., & Liberato, D. (2022). Learning by doing: Fostering tourism students' soft skills through interdisciplinarity and collaboration. In C. Silva, M. Oliveira & S. Silva (Eds), Proceedings of the 5th International Conference on Tourism Research, 2022 (pp. 441-448). Academic Conferences International Limited. https://papers.academic-conferences.org/index.php/ictr/article/view/119/278

WEF. (2023). Future of Jobs Report 2023. In Future of Jobs Report 2023 (Vol. 59, Issue April).

Author Biographies

Sandra Vasconcelos, Associate Professor (Polytechnic) at the School of Hospitality and Tourism, Polytechnic of Porto, Portugal. She holds a Master and a PhD in Multimedia in Education and is an integrated member of the Research Centre

"Didactics and Technology in Education of Trainers" and UNIAG – Applied Management Research Unit.

 **Carla Melo** is a Lecturer at the School of Hospitality and Tourism, Polytechnic of Porto, Portugal. She has a bachelor's degree in Tourism Management and Planning, and a master's in information management (Aveiro University, Portugal). Currently, she is developing her PhD research on Tourism Transformational Experiences, at Tilburg University (Netherlands).

 **António Melo**, Professor at the School of Hospitality and Tourism of Porto, member of CiTUR and collaborating member of CIDTFF. His educational background includes a Bachelor in Hotel Management, a master's degree in management and PhD in Education. António has 30 years of experience in hospitality and 20 years in academia.

 **Dália Liberato**, PhD in Tourism Management and Planning, from the University of Vigo, Spain. She is a Senior Lecturer at the School of Hospitality and Tourism (Polytechnic Institute of Porto), where she coordinates the Tourist Activities Management degree and Sustainability in Tourism and Hospitality master's degree.

 **Maria Carlos Lopes** has a PhD in Tourism from the University of Vigo (Spain). She is a Guest Senior Lecturer at the Lamego Higher School of Technology and Management (Polytechnic of Viseu) and also Director of the Degree in Tourism, Cultural and Heritage Management.

www.ingramcontent.com/pod-product-compliance
Lightning Source LLC
Chambersburg PA
CBHW072147160426
43197CB00012B/2280